DEEP STATE

THE MYSTERIOUS STATE WITHIN THE UNITED STATES

**Conversations
At a Seminar in a Parallel Universe**

SURENDRA KUMAR SAGAR

INDIA • SINGAPORE • MALAYSIA

Notion Press

Old No. 38, New No. 6
McNichols Road, Chetpet
Chennai - 600 031

First Published by Notion Press 2020
Copyright © Surendra Kumar Sagar 2020
All Rights Reserved.

ISBN 978-1-64783-641-2

ALSO BY SURENDRA KUMAR SAGAR

SIX WORDS

INTELLIGENT FIELD

BRIGHT LIGHT IN THE SKY

SWITCHED ON

CONTENTS

PREFACE

On planet Earth, in a certain parallel universe, something happened on September 11, 2001.

It looked like a plane striking one of the twin towers of the World Trade Center, New York. It was seen entering the building with apparently no reduction in its speed. Sometime later, another plane was seen striking the other tower. Like the first one, this too was seen entering the building with apparently no reduction in its speed.

The planes were seen changing shape and color; they were missing wings and were featureless and blurred. It was observed—by some experts—that the planes had no strobe lights. They didn't cast any shadows either.

The twin towers collapsed one by one.

The world was informed that it was a terrorist attack carried out by Al-Qaeda, who hijacked large planes—of the 757-767 class—and struck the two towers, one after the other. The 9/11 commission report investigated the matter and confirmed it was a terrorist attack.

Engineers, architects, expert pilots and many other professionals doubted the commission report but were ignored. Millions of innocent people died in the Middle East. Tens of thousands of American soldiers died as well.

Years later, a seminar entitled 'SWITCHED ON' was held at the National Institute of Advanced Studies, Bangalore…in that parallel universe, of course.

Albert Einstein (revised version): Can we say that Newton's third law has been violated?

Isaac Newton (RVO): It cannot be violated; it was never violated; it will never be violated.

A gentleman from the front row of the audience (the revised version of Sherlock Holmes): I have foolproof evidence, not of what happened on 9/11, but of what DID NOT HAPPEN, as was alleged to have occurred on 9/11. And that evidence lies in the statement, 'Newton's third law of motion cannot be violated'.

Albert Einstein (RV): Can we then say that there is a 'deep state' in America?

Deep State is all about what transpired during that seminar. It ultimately leads to 'stage-managing' the resignation of Donald Trump, in that parallel universe, of course.

Some of the characters in the play are dead scientists, such as Erwin Schrodinger, John Wheeler, Eugene Wigner, Albert Einstein, Leonardo Da Vinci, etc. The ones who are living are afraid of the 'deep state' of America and the world. They are playing it 'safe' and don't want to be involved.

But how do I bring the dead scientists to the stage?

Simple. I used the same trick I used in my first book, *Six Words*: I bring in the revised versions of these dead scientists. This all happens in a parallel universe, of course.

Recall a para from *Six Words*:

"In a certain parallel universe, there is a company called *REVISED GREATS INC0RPORATED*, located in Interlaken, Switzerland. This company creates (by selection and comprehensive training) revised versions of great scientists and philosophers of the past. These revised versions are mostly selected from retired Hollywood or Bollywood actors and are required to act how the original versions would have acted were they still alive. The actors should be fully aware of past events, including events that took place on Earth since the death of the original ones. The company then sends these great people (the revised ones) as consultants to various meetings, conferences, seminars, etc., wherever required. Profit, of course, is one of the motives. In some cases, such as Einstein, for example, there are several revisions (R1, R2, R3, etc.) available for deployment. It's a question of demand and supply."

Three other characters took part in a conversation that took place between commenters in response to a blog called *Can Black Holes Tell Us Something About Digital Computers?* It had been posted on Huffington Post on 1st August 2013 by the Scientist, Mario Livio. Two of these characters are Charlie Fox Trot and Diogenes of Alaska. These were pseudonyms of course. They have been retained as their actual names were not known to me. The third character was Surendra Kumar Sagar (yours truly), who wrote a significant response to the blog, suggesting that our universe was simulated and that it was a sort of super-consciousness that switched on the Big Bang of the current eon of the universe.

My response triggered a very lengthy and hugely interesting conversation between the three of us. Charlie strongly opposed my idea of a simulated universe and gave ample justification as to why he thought I was wrong. Diogenes of Alaska, though, did not oppose my idea. He wanted me to have a pragmatic approach on the subject and not be too carried away by such speculative ideas unless I had a reasonably firm grip on the totality of propositions entailed by what I put forward.

However, the idea of a simulated universe has gained considerable traction in recent times and several books have been written on the subject, notably *Information as the Nature of Reality*, which was edited by Paul Davies and Niels Henrik Gregerson. Another idea that is gaining some traction in recent times is panpsychism, the concept of a conscious universe via a proto-consciousness field. This, according to me, is nothing other than the intelligent field, which, incidentally, is the title of my second book.

Some time ago, I participated in a BBC playwriting competition for a 53-minute radio play. My entry was a play in two acts entitled, *Switched On*. The central idea was the suggestion that our universe was simulated and a kind of super-consciousness that switched on the Big Bang of the current eon of the universe. Arguments for and against this concept were discussed at length, both in the play and chapter five of my book, *Bright Light In The Sky*.

The primary 'hook' in the idea—in the context of the resolution of conflicts and wars on planet Earth—is the realization that 'simulation' is a preferred choice over 'randomness'. A simulation is necessary so that, as far as possible, everything happens in accordance with plans and designs to yield the desired results. In the case of the universe as a whole, the desired results are that life and consciousness should exist and flourish in various parts of the universe. In the case of human civilization, the desired results are peaceful coexistence, the avoidance of conflicts and wars with compassionate, able and responsible leaders at the helm of every country and that randomness should have little chance of getting in the way of the desired results.

All in all, it is to be ensured that men with an inadequate compassion and information index should have little chance of becoming leaders of nations.

⸻ • ● • ⸻

On the second day of the seminar, Leonardo Da Vinci (RVO) spearheaded the discussion on how intelligence can conquer unintelligence to bring about peace in the world. Scientists and philosophers, such as Erwin Schrodinger, Albert Einstein, John Wheeler, Immanuel Kant, Swami Vivekananda (all revised versions) and many others, provided their presentations on how to bring about a convergence of all religions into a single religion, which has the best chance of finding acceptance worldwide, leading to the end of conflicts and wars. Profound ideas, such as cosmic religious feeling, unity of consciousness, oneness of the mind, intelligent field (or the proto-consciousness field), infinite mind, the traveling cosmic mind, etc., emerged during the seminar. These ideas have the potential to add a significant, new dimension to the quest for knowledge on philosophy, religion, spirituality, humanism and other similar paths toward formulating an integrative view of life and the universe.

Finally, a consensus was reached: the future security of the human race should not be left to the revolving doors of chance. It must be planned meticulously with no scope for miscalculations. Just as the universe has immaculately designed constants of nature incorporated beautifully into the laws of science to enable life and consciousness to appear and understand the universe, in the same way, the actions of human beings (particularly of leaders of nations) should be meticulously designed to enable the continuation of this extraordinary intelligent life on this beautiful planet.

———•◆•———

That, of course, was what happened in a parallel universe. What happens in this universe remains to be seen. Like my other books, this too is an in-depth exploration of how humans can come together to change the course of history.

The ultimate objective is peace in the world.

The future is bright for the human race, provided we can survive the next few centuries and avoid self-destruction.

The deep future is even brighter for life and consciousness to flourish in the Cosmo with the kind help of an 'intelligent field' and the 'traveling cosmic mind'.

As you read on, some shocks may be encountered, which might lead to some turbulence of the mind. It is recommended you please fasten your seat belts.

SWITCHED ON

ACT 1

ENTER

CFT: Charlie Fox Trot

DOA: Diogenes of Alaska

AE: Albert Einstein (Revised Version)

ES: Erwin Schrodinger (RV)

JW: John Wheeler (RV)

EW: Eugene Wigner (RV)

LDV: Leonardo Da Vinci (RV)

SK: Surendra Kumar (Yours truly)

CFT: Recalling your words, SK, "And the current information shows the intelligent field to be severely contaminated and the only way to remove the contamination is by deleting the evil information and replacing it with good information." How do we do that?

SK: As we do in calculus, we first differentiate to understand the problem and then integrate to find the solution.

Let DOA, CFT and me do the differentiation part by providing all the information in the field on what has happening on planet Earth over the last hundred years or so and what cards are lying on the table, as per the current deal. Then we will ask the respected scientists assembled here to do the integration part, provide the solutions and tell us how to play the deal.

The information in the field has two categories: Category One corresponds to the information relating to events that actually happened, as recorded in history, beginning with Einstein's equation and continuing to the present day, which has some bearing on our current situation where we have more than 20,000 nuclear warheads located at several locations on the planet, not all of them in possession of safe hands.

I request DOA to please give his presentation on category one.

EW: What is category two?

SK: Category two corresponds to the information where there is a mismatch between the events that actually happened and those understood to have occurred as per recorded history.

[DOA started to give his presentation with a slide show to explain the full sequence of events that happened over the years, relating to the nuclear geo-politics of the world.

He spent about a couple of minutes to elaborate on each of the following:

EINSTEIN'S EQUATION AND THE DISCOVERY OF FISSION

THE RACE FOR SUPREMACY AND EINSTEIN'S LETTERS TO PRESIDENT ROOSEVELT

THE MANHATTAN PROJECT

THE BOMBING OF HIROSHIMA AND NAGASAKI AND THE AFTERMATH

NUCLEAR ARMS RACE

THE DOOMSDAY EMBLEMATIC CLOCK

PUGWASH CONFERENCES AND THE RUSSEL-EINSTEIN MANIFESTO

JOSEPH ROTBLAT

ABOUT THE BOOK, KEEPER OF THE NUCLEAR CONSCIENCE, BY ANDREW BROWN

THE 1962 CUBAN MISSILE CRISIS AND ITS AFTERMATH

THE ROLE OF PUGWASH IN THE RESOLUTION OF THE CUBAN MISSILE CRISIS

THE 1981 FIRST STRIKE SCENARIO

THE STRATEGIC DEFENSE INITIATIVE

SEPTEMBER 26, 1983—WORLD WAR 3 COULD HAVE STARTED

MIKHAEL GORBOCHOV'S POSITIVE APPROACH IGNORED BY THE UNITED STATES

THE NOBEL PEACE PRIZE OF 1995 TO ROTBLAT AND THE PUGWASH CONFERENCES

SWIMMING AGAINST THE CURRENT— RESPONSIBLE DISSIDENCE

ROTBLAT'S TEN POINT MEMO

THE WORLD OTHER THAN THE COLD WAR WORLD

THE KARGIL WAR OF 1999

THE 9/11 ATTACK ON THE WTC TOWERS

DOA played videos of the planes hitting the towers and went on to describe the event.]

DOA: On September 11, 2001, 19 Arab-Muslim hijackers took control of four commercial aircraft and used them as suicide weapons in a series of four coordinated acts of terrorism to strike the World Trade Center in New York City, the Pentagon in Arlington County, Virginia and an additional target in Washington DC. Two aircraft hit the World Trade Center while the third hit the Pentagon. A fourth plane never arrived at its destination, crashing in a field in Pennsylvania after a passenger revolt. The attack was carefully planned by Al-Qaeda, who sent 19 terrorists to take over the Boeing 757 and Boeing

767 aircraft, operated by American Airlines and United Airlines.

Osama Bin Laden was considered the chief planner and the mastermind behind the attacks. Motives for the attack include US support for Israel, Western support for attacking Muslims in Somalia, Russian atrocities against Muslims in Chechnya, Indian oppression against Muslims in Kashmir, Jewish aggression against Muslims in Lebanon, the presence of US troops in Saudi Arabia and sanctions against Iraq, etc.

Those were the stated objectives. There were also some Inferred objectives, such as **religious motivation**. Daniel Benjamin and Steven Simon, in their book, *The Age of Sacred Terror*, argue that the 9/11 terrorist attacks were purely religious. They are seen as "a sacrament...intended to restore to the universe a moral order that had been corrupted by the enemies of Islam". It was neither political nor strategic but an "act of redemption" meant to humiliate and slaughter those who defied the hegemony of God.

[At this stage, Albert Einstein interrupted the proceedings.]

AE: This is interesting to me. Did you say the planes were Boeing 757 and 767 aircraft operated by American Airlines and United Airlines?

DOA: Yes, those were the alleged planes.

AE: What do you mean by alleged?

DOA: I mean, as reported.

AE: They don't look that large to me. And how could they keep moving at the same speed, even after hitting the tower and disappearing completely into the building? If this is true, then I am afraid we may have to revise Newton's third law: For every action, there is an equal and opposite reaction. Try to imagine a tower moving at, say 400 miles per hour, hitting the flight 175. We would not expect the plane to be undamaged, leave aside disappear into the tower.

JW: I agree with AE. This is impossible. The bulk of the planes should have crumpled up and fallen to the ground soon after hitting the tower.

ES: In fact, they don't look like real planes to me, more like computer-generated stuff.

EW: It simply cannot happen without violating the established laws of science.

AE: What in the world is going on here?

DOA: I was coming to that. I understand there is a conspiracy theory, which is gaining appreciable ground recently, that the 9/11 attack on the WTC Towers was, in all probability, an inside job.

AE: What does Google tell us about this inside job?

CFT: I checked Google. Here is something of relevance. I will read it out for you:

"Possibly one of the most believed and widespread conspiracies has to do with the 9/11 attack in the United States. The United States government has been known (and proven) to have done a multitude of awful things, but usually, it is to countries other than their own.

There are demolitionists that claim that certain types of explosives made the towers fall. These people claim to be experts because they use these explosives weekly to take down other buildings.

There are so many glitches and things that just do not seem right about the 9/11 attack that it is hard to believe that it wasn't an inside job, especially in hindsight.

Many believe that the United States government planned this attack to inspire hatred toward Islam and, in turn, Iraq. This would result in the "War on Terror", which many just see as the "War of All the Oil We Can Take." Many American soldiers lost their lives because of this, along with many innocent civilians.

The world may be one step closer to finding the truth of this event. The government of Russia claims to have satellite images proving that the 9/11 attack was, in fact, an inside job. Putin is threatening the government with this information currently. There is no doubt this is causing mass panic in the White House. Hopefully, the American people will get their answers soon. God knows they deserve to know why so many of their people had to die."

AE: What do you have to say to this, SK, as a structural engineer? Will you please come forward and explain this?

SK: Sure, I will. I agree entirely with the great scientists assembled here. This could not have happened the way it is alleged to have happened without violating Newton's Laws of Science. Structural engineering is predominantly based on Newton's laws also.

AE: Please go ahead.

SK: To a structural engineer, a skyscraper is modeled as a large cantilever vertical column.

[Leonardo Da Vince, who was incidentally a structural engineer as well, asks a question.]

LDV: Can you tell us the dimensions and other details of the towers?

SK: Sure. Each tower was 64m square, standing 411m above street level and 21m below grade. The structural design comprised of a lightweight perimeter tube consisting of 244 exterior columns of 36 cm square steel box section spaced 1m c/c. Inside this outer tube, there was a massive 27m × 40m core made up of a framework of heavy columns, fully braced, which was designed to support the weight of the tower and, of course, the interconnecting beams. Steel beams 800 mm deep connected the core to the perimeter at each story. Concrete slabs were poured over these beams to form the floors.

We all know that the striking object pierced through and still, the structure didn't collapse immediately. It remained intact for quite some time before the 1000-degree temperature created the fall. Now, I'll ask you a question: Was that possible, considering the dimensions of the planes that were supposed to have hit the towers?

LDV: And what were these dimensions?

SK: First, consider the width: 156 feet for a Boeing 767, i.e., 47.5m wide. Now, we all know that the entire plane pierced through completely and settled down nicely inside the tower, which means as many as 47 out of 64 exterior columns were destroyed, which is about 73%. By no means is it just a handful. So what do we get? 73% of the exterior columns destroyed and the structure is still standing. Were the remaining 17 or 18 exterior columns overdesigned to such an extent that they took care of the workload of the 47 columns that 'died'? Or was it that the beams connecting the inner core structure to the exterior columns were also designed as cantilevers, projecting from the inner core.

Next, consider the length—159 feet for a Boing 767, i.e., 48.5m long. As mentioned earlier, there is a central massive inner core in the tower comprising of heavy and cross-braced columns and beams. This massive inner core of columns was impossible to pierce through by the plane, which must have considerably lost speed soon after striking the exterior columns, not to mention the heavy RCC floor slabs and the joists connecting the inner core to the exterior columns. And if we are supposed to believe that the plane indeed pierced through the inner core after comprehensively violating Newton's laws, wouldn't the tower have immediately collapsed after several of the inner core columns were eliminated?

Hence, it is abundantly clear that the plane could not have reached the inner core before coming to rest, which means that the maximum distance the plane traveled after it struck the tower's external columns and reached the edge of the inner core is no more than 60 feet, which means as much as about 99 feet of the plane ought to have remained outside the tower, broken off, crumpled up and gone crumbling to the ground below. It would be a more or less similar case for the other tower.

LDV: Nicely explained, SK. Additionally, there is a torsional effect. The instant the wings touched the steel, a torsional force would have been exerted on them. The velocity of the ends of the wings would have been substantially reduced; there is no way they could have sliced steel.

SK: Thank you.

AE: What is the opinion of expert pilots on this? Could a terrorist—no matter how hard he trained—have maneuvered the plane in such a precise manner?

CFT: Here is an expert pilot's view. In fact, it's the same pilot who flew the actual aircraft involved in 9/11, on other days, of course.

"I flew the two aircraft involved in 9/11—flight number 175 and 93. 757 allegedly went down in Shanksville and 175 allegedly hit the South Tower. I don't believe a so-called terrorist can train on a [Cessna] 172 and then jump in a cockpit of a 757-767 class plane and vertically and laterally navigate the aircraft, fly it at speeds exceeding its design limit by well over 100 knots, make high-speed high-banked turns and exceed probably 5, 6, 7 G's. The aircraft would literally fall out of the sky. I couldn't do it and I'm absolutely positive they couldn't do it. For a guy to just jump into the cockpit and fly like an ace is impossible. There is not one chance in a million." said Wittenberg, recalling that when he made the jump from Boeing 727's to the highly sophisticated computerized characteristics of the 737's through 767's, it took him considerable time to feel comfortable flying.

The airplane could not have flown at the speeds they said it did without going into what they call a high-speed stall. The aircraft won't go that fast if you start pulling those high G maneuvers at those bank angles...To expect this alleged airplane to run these maneuvers with a total amateur at the controls is simply ludicrous..."It's roughly a 100-ton airplane. And an airplane that weighs 100 tons all assembled is still going to have 100 tons of disassembled trash and parts after it hits a building. There was no wreckage from a 757 at the Pentagon...The vehicle that hit the

Pentagon was not Flight 77. We think, as you may have heard before, it was a cruise missile."

AE: Good job, CFT. Can you please provide some more expert views?

CFT: Yes, here is another expert view.

"The alleged flight 175 is seen intersecting with eight floors that consisted of steel trusses connected at one end to the core columns at the other, where each floor was covered with 4-8" of concrete, representing an acre of concrete apiece and posing enormous horizontal resistance to any airplane's penetration into the building.

In some of the impact videos, we see what we are told is a plane cartoonishly pass through the steel face of the tower like a ghost. As the alleged plane makes contact with the tower, there is no bending, buckling or breaking of the plane. No wings breaking or other parts of the plane breaking apart. This is impossible. It is cartoon physics. It melts into the side of the tower like a knife through butter. A passenger jet is a hollow aluminum and plastic tube which is highly vulnerable to impacts with flying birds. The 'plane' we are told is flight 175 is depicted as being simultaneously both half in the South Tower and still completely intact, if a pair of the plane's fuselage hits the steel exterior of the South Tower, the fuselage should be breaking up. That would cause the wings to break off.

From the holes left in both towers after 'impact', we are supposed to believe that the wings sliced clean through the 14-inch steel beams, but this is simply impossible. The fragile, mostly hollow, aluminum wings would not slice through all the 14-inch steel box columns of the WTC Towers and leave a Wylie Coyote style hole. An airplane wing can be sliced in half by a wooden telephone pole.

Apart from one or two props placed there, like a bit of tire and a few engine parts that didn't even match a Boing 767 and like the laughable bit of engine on the Pentagon lawn, there were no real plane parts or debris to be seen and no black boxes were ever found at ground zero. In reality, if a plane had hit the tower, it would have crushed up like a car hitting a wall and its wings would have broken off and the majority of the plane would have fallen to the street below. The street below would have been littered with plane debris and the charred remains of the passengers, yet it wasn't because there was no plane.

NO OFFICIAL CRASH REPORTS: FAA Regulation 121 requires a comprehensive investigation of all crashes of scheduled commercial flights, yet there are no official crash reports on the four incidents because there were no planes.

PLANES HAVE A CGI APPEARANCE: In all of the footage released, the alleged planes hitting the twin towers clearly do not look real. The planes have a computer-generated appearance. In different footage, we see the planes are changing shape and color, missing wings and are featureless and blurred. Pilot John Lear made the observation that the plane has no strobe lights. They also casted no shadows.

According to BTS statistics, both 11 and 77 officially never took off on 9/11. The meticulous data kept on every airliner taking-off at every airport in the country also showed no elapsed run-way time, wheels-off time and taxi-out time, not to mention several other categories left blank on 9/11 concerning the two flights. Although flights 11 and 77 have the above data meticulously logged on 9/10, it was suspiciously absent on 9/11, even when every other plane that took off that day had been recorded and logged by the BTS. The flight that was labeled flight 11 by air traffic control was ten miles from Manhattan at 8.46 am. If flights AA 11 and AA 77 never existed, then there are only two planes, not four, to be accounted for.

Investigators who have checked the tail numbers for the planes that departed as UA 93 and UA 175 on 9/11 (namely N591UA and N612UK respectively) believe that these planes are still in service. If so, and if AA 11 and AA 77 never existed, then the number of Boeing 757s and 767s destroyed on 9/11 was not four, as the US government maintains, but rather zero. Both UA 175, plane number N612UA and UA 93, plane number N591UA, were still registered and valid more than four years after (their) alleged destruction."

AE: What is the current status of these conspiracy theories?

DOA: They have been making waves for quite some time. Recently, they started gaining ground appreciably. But it is also true that they have been DEBUNKED by scientific studies and eyewitnesses.

EW: Why was the investigation left incomplete? What is stopping the debunkers and the conspiracy theorists from coming together in a conference, analyzing the whole thing, coming to a consensus and then informing the world what happened?

AE: That is the question.

DOA: Incidentally, there is an American non-profit organization called **Architects & Engineers for 9/11 Truth** that promotes the controlled demolition conspiracy theory disputing accepted conclusions around the September 11 attacks, including the 9/11 Commission Report. Founded in 2006, the group calls for "a truly independent investigation" into the September 11 attacks as they believe government agency investigations into the collapse of the World Trade Center did not address what it calls "massive evidence for explosive demolition".

EW: What is the current strength of the group?

DOA: I don't have the latest info, but in August 2018, the group had over 25000 members, including over 3000 architects and engineers.

EW: What about professional bodies of architects and engineers, including aerospace engineers? Do they support these theories?

DOA: I think they have chosen not to debate proponents of these theories. Perhaps, they do not want to lend them credibility or simply stay away from getting involved.

JW: Is that the reason we have been invited to this seminar?

SK: *[After much thinking]*: Yes.

EW: So how do we reconcile and make sense of it? I mean who from America could have benefited from the whole thing?

JW: I think I have a theory that explains what might have happened. I hope I am wrong.

EW: And what's that?

JW: First off, recall the Vietnam War and the assassination of John F. Kennedy, who was planning to end the war, and the conspiracy theory that he was killed by the owners of major corporations who benefited from the war's continuation.

In the Vietnam War, the leaders of the White House claimed at the time that it was a necessary and crucial war.

When Kennedy took over the presidency and deviated from the general line of policy drawn up for the White House and wanted to stop this unjust war, this angered—big time—the owners of the major corporations who benefited from its continuation. And so Kennedy was killed. The Al-Qaeda wasn't present at that time, but rather, those corporations were the primary beneficiary of his killing. The war continued after that for approximately one decade, even though it was clear to one and all that it was an unjust and unnecessary war.

Over the years, decades rather, the Military-Industrial Complex of the US of A, comprising of these major—not to mention powerful—corporations, including defense contractors, have been stage-managing the US Foreign Policy in a way that ensures business as usual for the MIC.

SK: I agree entirely. In fact, someone commented during a conversation with me in response to a blog on Huffington Post, several years back:

"The Dept of Defense (DOD) is the 'Republican Welfare System'—Defense contracts are bid on and let through a multitude of Contracting Offices—with very lucrative amounts being agreed to. Most of these businesses are Republican owned. Billions of dollars every year for goods and services. Contracting out is a big Republican policy. Of course, you have to have a war for this to really be 'profitable'."

JW: Manufacturing arms, ammunition and weapons of mass destruction and exporting them to nations in conflict—sometimes to both parties—thus increasing the conflict, has been at the center stage of American foreign policy. I am thinking, some—perhaps a single-digit number—members of the group. When these major corporations of the so-called Military-Industrial Complex, with or without the knowledge/consent of the supreme boss, came to know of the terrorists' plans, they decided to secretly join hands with them.

"Two can dig better than one." (Remember the dialogue from *The Good, the Bad, the Ugly*.)

Later, as the situation got more and more complex, the number of conspirators may have increased significantly. The entire operation was done under a shroud of secrecy.

EW: That was no big deal. Compare this with the Manhattan Project, which had 130000 people on board, where the entire operation was carried out in complete secrecy.

I'm just guessing, but I think the two planes that hit the WTC Towers were specially designed small planes loaded with massive explosives. They were either remote-controlled or manned by – Oh, what do I know!

Or maybe, a computer-generated show timed simultaneously with an explosive blast in the basement. An abs-controlled demolition of the building! What do I know!

All I can say—by intuition of course—is that the job was made much easier for the terrorists.

DOA: The end result was in line with the desired expectations of the participants in the crime: revenge for the terrorists against the Americans, a sharp adrenaline rush for many hard-line Muslims on hearing about the killing of thousands of non-Muslims and a stupendous plethora of business opportunities for the Military-Industrial Complex of the United States of America.

EW: Let the presentation continue from where we left.

DOA: Sure. The intelligent field on planet Earth was severely contaminated. The Middle East faced catastrophic wars, including civil wars. Millions of Muslims died and tens of thousands of American soldiers died. More than 17 years later, the crisis in the Middle East is far from over. As long as the Shias and the Sunnis of the Muslim world keep fighting with each other, the Western World (particularly the US) will keep exploiting them.

EW: The slide show, please. Continue the sequence.

DOA: Sure.

THE 2003 SYMPOSIUM ON SCIENCE AND BEYOND IN INDIA AND PROF. M. S. SWAMINATHAN'S MESSAGE

CHARLES TOWNES' VIEWS ON SCIENCE AND RELIGION

AMERICAN INTERFERENCES CONTINUE IN THE MIDDLE EAST

THE BUSH INVASION OF IRAQ IN 2003 AND ITS CONSEQUENCES

DOA: In the words of Rotblat, "Neither of the three reasons advanced for the launch of the attacks (to eliminate Saddam's weapons of mass destruction, to destroy the link with Al-Qaeda and to overthrow a bad regime) was acceptable to the world. The main reason was that the United States was pursuing global dominance intermittently since the Second World War. From the very beginning, the development of nuclear weapons was used to give the United States a dominant position in the world. In the beginning, they were determined not to allow any other nation have nuclear weapons."

Rotblat believed that President Bush's disregard for arms control treaties, coupled with an interest in developing new nuclear warheads, threatened the progress that had been made in nuclear disarmament over the previous two decades. Regarding morality and equity in world affairs, Rotblat stated the following:

"It is the United States that has to be called to order. It is intolerable that in this day and age, the mightiest country in the world should have declared that its overriding motivation in international affairs was the self-interest of the United States of America. I cannot help the feeling that selfishness and greed—which became the driving force after the victory of capitalism in the ideological struggle—are, to some extent, responsible for the terrible carnage that we have just witnessed."

AMERICAN INTERFERENCES CONTINUED.

AE: Once, America was considered as the best place in the world. I remember saying this: "It has an international psyche. It constitutes the bulwark of the democratic way of life; it has demonstrated that individual freedom provides a better basis for productive labor than any form of tyranny and its political and economic position is so powerful that it can help the world by breaking the tradition of war from which the world suffered."

But I am afraid to say that all that has changed now.

DOA: Yes, having become rich and powerful, America also became selfish and arrogant: Selfish in the sense that it started grabbing a disproportionately higher share of the world's resources and arrogant in the sense that, in order to ensure the safety and security of its own people, America began to undertake large-scale interference in the affairs of other countries. This interference was manipulated to create rifts between nations interfered with or between two segments of the same nation with which America interfered. To add insult to injury, America turned a blind eye to these rifts.

ISLAMIC FUNDAMENTALIST EXTREMISM

DOA: American interferences in the Middle East, where they preferred dictatorships to secular liberal democracies (so that it is easy for dictators to align with common causes and grab the resources of a country), is responsible for the disenchantment of the common people in these countries and consequent unrest. It's an established fact that the United States, with the help of Israel, did not allow secular nationalism to prevail in many countries in the Middle East. Instead, they destroyed secular nationalism, which helped create Islamic fundamentalist extremism.

CIVIL WARS IN IRAQ AND SYRIA

CREATION AND RISE OF ISIS

DOA: The Bush invasion resulted in tens of thousands of civilian casualties. Friends and relatives of those killed in the Sunni faction became terrorists, so it became a justification to fight them; a government and a local army were installed to fight remnant terrorism. This army was predominantly made up of another faction—Shias—but it had several Sunnis, too. At the behest of the Bush government, the Sunnis were thrown out of the Iraqi Army. They had no jobs and nowhere to go. They became victims of time, caused by the interactions of the world.

When the American forces withdrew from Iraq, which turned out to be a great error of judgment by Barack Obama, those of them who were in possession of weapons became terrorists. Others in their faction acquired weapons and joined them; others did not join them as fighters but simply supported them. They took control of large areas of Iraq as well as Syria. They are called ISIS. There is nothing religious about them or their actions. As explained earlier, they are all made up of disgruntled people, insecure and unhappy victims of time caused by the interactions of the world. They picked up disgruntled young people from all over the world, mostly from Europe; they sympathize with them and entice them to join them.

If the essence of religion, any religion, is to "live and let live" and to live in peace and harmony, then there is nothing religious in what they do. But they do take advantage of the contradictions in their religious document, which according to their own interpretations, permits them to indulge in jihad against non-Muslims. If they die, a place in heaven is promised to them by their leaders. It's a natural selection virus called "to live and let die" that enters minds and causes conflicts and wars. It has infected the minds of the leaders and they are injecting the virus into the minds and bodies of normal, innocent human beings in such a way as to create a different kind of virus called "to die and let die".

ENOUGH IS ENOUGH. RUSSIA AND CHINA START PREPARING FOR CONFRONTATION WITH US.

DOA: I will ask CFT to gather all the information on this severe development and enlighten us on the subject.

[After a short coffee break, CFT provided the required info.]

CFT: Decades-long American interferences in the Middle East and other countries, the 9/11 inside job, the Bush Invasion in Iraq, the civil wars in Iraq and Syria, the US support for the rebels in Syria (where Al-Qaeda happened to be on the same side of the court as the US), etc., created a firm impression where America was seen by Russia and China, and by most of the rest of the world, as an insane bully that meddled with everything on the international stage.

China and Russia decided to start preparing for the ultimate confrontation with the US of A.

> *"China started building a modern and regionally powerful navy with a limited but growing capability for conducting operations beyond China's near-seas region. China's improving naval capabilities posed a potential challenge in the Western Pacific to the US Navy's ability to achieve and maintain control of blue-water ocean areas in wartime—the first such challenge the US Navy has faced since the end of the Cold War.*
>
> *China's naval modernization efforts encompassed a broad array of platform and weapon acquisition programs, including anti-ship ballistic missiles (ASBMs), anti-ship cruise missiles (ASCMs), submarines, surface ships, aircraft and supporting C4ISR (command and control, communications, computers, intelligence, surveillance, and reconnaissance) systems.*

China is fielding an ASBM equipped with a maneuverable reentry vehicle designed to hit moving ships at sea. China, in other words, has weapons capable of destroying US aircraft carriers, destroyers and other ships within a range of 1,500-kilometers."

In August (2015), the Chinese and Russians held their largest naval joint exercise in history, featuring scores of warships, hundreds of troops and an amphibious landing, in what appeared to be a deepening of ties meant to counter a rising US military presence in Asia.

In September 2015, Chinese warships were spotted operating near the coast of Alaska. This was reported across the mainstream media.

> *"In response to that territorial provocation, the US Navy sent the USS Lassen destroyer to within 12 nautical miles of China's newly-constructed military bases in the Spratly Islands. China's communist government openly condemned the act as a provocation of war and warned that Beijing would 'never allow any country to violate China's territorial waters and airspace in the name of protecting freedom of navigation and overflight'."*

The mainstream media on either side, with a few exceptions, did not report any of the above developments. They wrote what they were asked to write.

AE: Curious…

CFT: *"Right now, the United States and China are in an undeclared state of war. China stands ready to strike* *the United States with nuclear warheads or high-altitude EMP weapons that would destroy the US power grid and cause casualties in the range of 90 percent across the unprepared population.*

Many people believe that China and Russia are working together to prepare for a massive first strike against the United States that would cripple its defenses and economy. Following that first strike, a land invasion would commence, using Russian troops.

Supporting this theory, Russian submarines have been spotted near undersea internet cables in an obvious effort to document their whereabouts so that the cables can be instantly severed, unleashing a devastating blow to the US economy. Russian submarines and spy ships are aggressively operating near the vital undersea cables that carry almost all global internet communications, raising concerns among some American military and intelligence officials that the Russians might be planning to attack those lines in times of conflict."

In times of tension or conflict, the ultimate Russian hack on the United States could involve severing the fiber-optic cables at some of their hardest-to-access locations to halt the instant communications on which the West's governments, economies and citizens have grown dependent.

BRIGHT LIGHT IN THE SKY

CFT: Sometime in early November 2015, as reported by BBC, people in California saw a mysterious bright light in the sky. The flare rose high in the air, and then a wide, bright and blue flash emerged in a cone shape. The display could be seen for several minutes. Pretty soon, videos were posted on-line and sent Californians into a panic.

"Social media was flooded with theories and people were asking questions. Was it a comet or meteors, a nuclear missile attack or even a nuclear bomb? Some people knew that a day earlier to the phenomenon, the Federal Aviation Authorities had issued flight restrictions for the LA International Airport denying aircraft access to one of the most frequent approach paths for international and domestic travel.

The official explanation made available soon thereafter was that the US Navy launched a test missile just because they 'routinely' test missiles.

The media in California confirmed that the light came from an unarmed Trident missile fired from the USS Kentucky navy submarine. But there was no way for the media to know whether this missile was really unarmed or not, as the sole source on that question is the US Navy itself."

Why was this necessary?

DOA: My guess is that it was a $31 million billboard telling Russia and China, "Don't meddle (....) with us."

In fact, it was a thermonuclear missile launch near Los Angeles—a final sign of World War III on the precipice; the US, China and Russia all escalating covert attacks in run-up to global war.

"If you put the pieces of the puzzle together, what's really shaping up was a massive, multi-layered preemptive strike against America, an empire—as said before—seen by the rest of the world as an insane bully that meddles with everything on the international stage. This first strike, combining the forces and expertise of both China and Russia, may consist of the following:

1. *High-altitude EMP detonation over North America, destroying regional power grids.*

2. *A devastating currency war initiated by China announcing its own gold-backed currency while dumping US Treasury debt on the open market.*

3. *A Russian-led severing of undersea fiber-optic cables.*

4. *Russian-launched nuclear missiles targeting US coastal cities.*

5. *A China-led assault on US Navy warships using anti-ship ballistic missiles (ASBMs).*

6. *A cyber warfare attack on key US infrastructures, including water delivery systems, nuclear power plants and the power grid.*

As all this was going on, the Obama Administration was firing all the top military commanders who knew how to survive such an assault.

Congress heard testimony that the United States is not ready for World War III while Russia is chomping at the bit to "get it on". Further, Congress has learned that Obama has been once again badly outmaneuvered by Putin, the master chess player. The Chinese and the Russians were all set to kick America's rear end in the upcoming war."

EW: But the war didn't start then. What happened?

CFT: Surprising. I have no idea. Perhaps it can still happen.

EW: I'm curious. Can anyone explain?

AE: Perhaps it was realized, via the intelligent field, and wondered why the common man in America should be punished? Why not just take care of the DEEP STATE of America?

EW: What do you mean by 'the deep state of America'?

AE: It is just a short form that includes the MIC, the defense contractors, the major corporations, some wealthy people, some highly senior bureaucrats who don't leave, even after the presidents go, some adventure seekers and so on.

EW: You mean those responsible for the 9/11 inside job?

AE: That's right. As well as those responsible for the Kennedy assassination.

EW: So what would have been the planning—the mindset—of Putin and co.?

JW: They probably thought, "Let's wait for some time and see who the next president of the US is."

EW: And maybe…stage-manage to put the right one in?

JW: Very likely, that might have been the plan.

EW: Was Putin (& co.) successful in this 'stage-management'?

JW: Yes, of course. He is from Russia. They are good chess players.

EW: So Donald Trump was considered the right choice against 'the deep state'?

JW: Between the two finalists, yes.

EW: Why? What was the problem with Hillary Clinton? Was she with the deep state?

JW: No, but she was not expected to be able to control it (or avoid being controlled by it). Besides, she was too dangerous for Putin (& co.).

EW: Was Donald Trump expected to be successful against the 'DS'?

JW: Yes, he's expected to be, with the kind help of Putin (& co.).

EW: Was the plan successful…for anyone?

JW: For Putin (& co.), it was, but only to a small extent. For the rest of the world and for the US, I have to say, it's a big 'NO'. I think Trump made a complete mess of everything. To the problems created by the deep state, the problems created by the Corrupt State of Donald Trump were added.

SK: It was expected to be 'Donald Trump vs. the deep state', but it turned out to be 'Donald Trump + the deep state'.

DOA: We are closer to a nuclear war than at any stage in the past, ever since World War II.

CFT: And the 'DS' is still in control I think.

AE: We'll see about that. Don't worry.

JW: As they say, "Have no fear when Einstein is here."

EW: So what do we do?

JW: Let DOA complete the presentation on the information in the field.

[They break for lunch and soon reassemble on the stage.

DOA resumes his presentation.]

THE TWO YEARS ENDING DECEMBER 2018

DOA: Donald Trump won the US Election in November 2016. He considers Putin to be a great friend. Trump and Putin have been mutually admiring and continuously praising each other for quite some time. Following Trump's election, Putin found no difficulty in helping Assad and the Syrian government forces in closing in and finally retaking Aleppo from the rebels. But the civil war in Syria is far from over. As long as the Sunnis are in majority in Syria, they will not like to be ruled by a Shia-led government; the unrest may continue unless and until the two factions unite.

The CIA has found out about Russia's role in successfully manipulating the US elections to ensure that Trump was elected. Obama is furious and called for an investigation. Some people consider this interference by Russia, which is extremely serious, of the same magnitude of seriousness as the Pearl Harbor or the 9/11 attack.

Trump offended China big time by warming up to the Taiwan President.

He indicated he may not support Iran's nuclear deal with the US and other countries, which infuriated Iran. The equation became extremely complex.

Putin's capacity as a 'master chess player' to manipulate and outmaneuver and Trump's lack of knowledge and understanding of what's going on in the world did not—at *that stage—auger well for peace in the world.*

Donald Trump, during his election campaign, spelled out his intent in bringing about some changes that, as per him, could make America great again. But the same changes, according to the general world opinion, could endanger world peace, including peace in America.

The big news as 2016 ended—before Trump was installed as POTUS—was that the UN passed a resolution for a Two-State solution of the Israel-Palestine issue. The resolution was passed with 14 votes in favor and none against. The US abstained and did not veto this. The US Secretary of State, John Kerry, delivered a stunning speech on 28th December 2016 that lasted for 70 minutes. Kerry strongly defended the

US decision to allow a UN resolution condemning Israeli settlements, saying if Washington had vetoed it, Israel would have been given a license for "unfettered settlement construction" and the end of the peace process. Israeli Prime Minister, Benjamin Netanyahu, strongly criticized the resolution as well as the Obama Administration and made his intentions clear by saying he will not abide by the resolution. Donald Trump also criticized the resolution. He supported Netanyahu and told him not to worry and that 20th January 2017 (the date fixed for taking over as president) was fast approaching.

In January 2017, the Doomsday Emblematic Clock was moved by 30 seconds to two and a half minutes to midnight.

Donald Trump visited Saudi Arabia and met with the leaders of the nations—all Sunnis—friendly with Saudi Arabia. He danced with them and established a relationship that would enable him to sell billions of dollars' worth of arms, which was intended to be used against Iran, of course, when the time came.

AE: The deep state influence, I guess. Go on.

DOA: ICAN (International Campaign to Abolish Nuclear Weapons) was awarded the Nobel Prize for peace for its work to draw attention to the catastrophic humanitarian consequences of any use of nuclear weapons and for its ground-breaking efforts to achieve a treaty-based prohibition of such weapons. The UN Nuclear Weapon Ban Treaty (NBT) was adopted in July 2017.

A Nuclear-Free World or Nuclear-Weapon World?

CFT: *Nuclear-armed states, and especially the United States, exercised considerable pressure on other states not to sign the NBT. Sweden was a case in point: the US Defense Secretary Mattis directly threatened Sweden not to sign the NBT. Otherwise, Sweden's defense cooperation and eventual NATO membership would be at risk. It appeared that nuclear-armed states were, indeed, worried about the NBT and this in itself was a sign that the NBT mattered.*

As pointed out by Dr. Ruff (Founder of ICAN), humanity is currently at a crossroads. One lane is leading to a nuclear-free world, and the NBT is one of the tools needed to achieve that purpose. The other lane is a world in which states continue to possess nuclear weapons. He drew attention to serious tensions between NATO and Russia, the US and China and in several parts of the world, such as in Ukraine, the Middle East and Southeast Asia. At the same time, nuclear threats and the intention to use these weapons were openly affirmed not only by the US and Russia but also by others such as the UK's PM, Theresa May, and by India and Pakistan. The continued existence of nuclear weapons is strengthened by the significant underlying arms industry and the enormous governmental investments therein: globally, annual expenditure on nuclear weapons was estimated at US $105 billion—or $12 million an hour. Dr. Ruff concludes that there is currently no commitment to nuclear disarmament evident among the nuclear-armed states and their accomplices.

The Situation in Northeast Asia

DOA: The dangers related to North Korean nuclear activities turned serious in terms of possible use of nuclear weapons by them.

Donald Trump came out with a barrage of extremely provocative statements against North Korea, apart from signaling his intent. In a United Nations meeting, he indicated that he wanted to totally destroy North Korea. A few examples of his provocative words:

> *"North Korea best not make any more threats to the United States. They will be met with fire and fury like the world has never seen. Kim Jong Un has been very threatening, beyond a normal statement. And as I said, they will be met with fire, fury, and frankly, power, the likes of which this world has never seen before."*

> *"The era of strategic patience with the North Korean Regime has failed. Many years, and it's failed, and frankly, that patience is over."*

Trump's reckless and hazardous approach emboldened Kim further and placed South Korea in a deep fix. Trump made it clear that he cared only about US interests. To continue kowtowing to Washington would be dangerous, even if Seoul cannot entirely quit the pretense of honoring its long-time ally, at least not yet. Indeed, the Trump presidency, less than a year old, had been a headache for President Moon, who won the elections in May, promising greater engagement and an end to hostility between the two Koreas. He took power exactly as Trump engaged in a verbal escalation with Pyongyang, threatening "fire and fury" and unilateral military action against North Korea.

Kim Jon Un, emboldened by Trump, declared his intent on pursuing his goal of reaching that ultimate capacity to hit the US Mainland wherever he wants. On Wednesday, the 29th of November 2017, North Korea launched another ICBM that could reach the American mainland. A Korean news agency reported: *"With this system, the DPRK has become possessed of another new-type inter-continental ballistic rocket weaponry system, capable of carrying a super-heavy nuclear warhead and attacking the whole mainland of the US."*

US defense chief, James Mattis, confirmed the missile launch was unprecedented. *"It went higher than any previous shot they've taken. It's a research-and-development effort on their part to continue to build ballistic missiles, to threaten everywhere in the world, basically."*

Donald Trump's response: *"Additional major sanctions will be imposed. This situation will be handled. America has made clear that it has lost faith in the effectiveness of diplomacy when dealing with Kim Jong Un's communist regime."*

Kim Jon Un's response was: *"The Nuclear Button is right here on my table."*

Donald Trump's response: *"It is on my table too and it's a much bigger Nuclear Button…And it works."*

In the Pentagon, senior officers knew that an attack on North Korea could lead to the deaths of hundreds of thousands—in South Korea as well as the North—and trigger unfathomable global instability. They have reluctantly concluded, however, that a pre-emptive US military strike and regime change might be the least worst of a menu.

Where will it all lead to? That was the question.

On January 25, 2018, the Bulletin of Atomic Scientists placed the needle of the emblematic clock at two minutes to midnight. The closest since 1953.

CFT: A small extract from the statement explaining the resetting the time on the doomsday clock:

> *"In the past year, US allies have needed reassurance about American intentions more than ever. Instead, they have been forced to negotiate a thicket of conflicting policy statements from a US Administration weakened in its cadre of foreign policy professionals, suffering from turnover in senior leadership, led by an undisciplined and disruptive president, and unable to develop, coordinate, and clearly communicate a coherent nuclear policy. This inconsistency constitutes a major challenge for deterrence, alliance management, and global stability. It has made the existing nuclear risks greater than necessary and added to their complexity."*

UPDATE AS ON APRIL 2018

DOA: There WAS another chemical attack on the city of Douma on the outskirts of Damascus, in Syria, killing about 40 civilians. Russia and Syria have denied any involvement by the Syrian Government forces.

A few days later, the US, Britain and France carried out surgical strikes on Syrian targets—presumably factories and establishments making chemical weapons—in retaliation for the chemical attacks. There is worldwide criticism of these surgical strikes, though some countries, notably Japan, Germany and Australia, supported the action.

Russia, Iran and Syria have started proclaiming victory against the rebels and their supporters. They think the war is over, but the US and UK are trying to say, "It's not over yet."

Questions are being asked: "Is there a bomb that is not chemical?", "Is it ok to kill millions using conventional weapons, but not ok to kill a few dozen who are rebels against the ruling government (hence equivalent to terrorists) by chemical weapons?"

Trump and the North Korean leader, Kim Jong Un, are likely to meet in May/June to discuss denuclearization by Kim.

CIA Director, Pompeo, has already held a secret meeting with the North Korean leader, Kim Jong Un. North Korea and South Korea prepare for their own summit on April 27, with a bid to formally end the 1950-53 Korean War being a major factor in talks. Such discussions between the two Koreas, and North Korea and the United States, would have been unthinkable at the end of last year, after months of escalating tension and fear of war over the North's weapons programs.

North Korea and South Korea met on April 27, 2018 and signed the Panmunjom Declaration of Peace, Prosperity and Unification of the Korean Peninsula. The document commits the two countries to a nuclear-free peninsula and talks to bring a formal end to the Korean War. The leaders ended the summit with a formal dinner and a toast.

Many world leaders were moved by the Korean leaders coming together. The UN General Secretary applauded the historic Korean summit and noted that many around the world were deeply impressed and moved by the powerful imagery.

EVENTS DURING MAY 2018

The month of May 2018 witnessed some events of far-reaching significance. The needle of the 'Doomsday Emblematic Clock' would have seen some wild fluctuations had it been monitored on a daily basis.

Donald Trump Withdraws from the Paris Agreement on Climate Change

CFT: President Donald Trump announced his intention to withdraw from the Paris Agreement on Climate Change. The president claimed that the agreement was a bad deal for America. The reality is that his disavowal of the treaty is putting the United States increasingly at odds with the rest of the world and harming Americans.

Fundamentally, there is no reason this administration should want to rework the Paris deal. The agreement did not impose undue burdens on the United States, as the president claimed, but allowed it and every other country to determine their own emission-reduction targets and create their own plans to increase ambition over time. All evidence suggested that the president was wrong in claiming that adhering to our target would hurt the US' economy and destroy jobs. He was also wrong in claiming that the agreement allowed large developing countries like China to do nothing to cut their emissions until 2030. In reality, China has already made significant strides to decarbonize its economy and is on pace to achieve its Paris targets by 2030. Similarly, India now has some of the most ambitious renewable energy targets on Earth and is on track to meet them.

Since the president's announcement, this landmark pact aimed at tackling climate change has only gained traction. No other country is signaling it will follow the United States' lead in withdrawing. Meanwhile, thousands of American businesses, cities, states and organizations are ramping up efforts in an attempt to help fill the gap.

Donald Trump Pulls out of the Iran Nuclear Deal

Except for a few countries, such as Israel and Saudi Arabia, the entire world condemned US President's decision to pull out of the Iran Nuclear Deal.

Former President, Barack Obama, slammed President Trump's decision to withdraw from the Iran nuclear agreement that he helped negotiate.

CFT: The world opinion is reflected in Obama's statement, made on Tuesday (8th May 2018). An extract from the same is reproduced below:

"There are few issues more important to the security of the United States than the potential spread of nuclear weapons, or the potential for even more destructive war in the Middle East."

In 2015, Obama and former Secretary of State, John Kerry, brokered the so-called Joint Comprehensive Plan of Action, limiting Tehran's nuclear program.

> *"The reality is clear," Obama said on Tuesday, "The JCPOA is working—that is a view shared by our European allies, independent experts, and the current US Secretary of Defense. The JCPOA is in America's interest—it has significantly rolled back Iran's nuclear program. And the JCPOA is a model for what diplomacy can accomplish—its inspections and verification regime is precisely what the United States should be working to put in place with North Korea.*

> *"Indeed, at a time when we are all rooting for diplomacy with North Korea to succeed, walking away from the JCPOA risks losing a deal that accomplishes—with Iran—the very outcome that we are pursuing with the North Koreans." The former president continued. "That is why today's announcement is so misguided. Walking away from the JCPOA turns our back on America's closest allies and an agreement that our country's leading diplomats, scientists, and intelligence professionals negotiated. In a democracy, there will always be changes in policies and priorities from one administration to the next. But the consistent flouting*

of agreements that our country is a party to risks eroding America's credibility, and puts us at odds with the world's major powers."

Stressing that policy "debates in our country should be informed by facts", Obama detailed six "facts", noting that the agreement was reached after building an international coalition that included the United Kingdom, France, Germany, the European Union, Russia, China, and Iran; it has succeeded in "rolling back Iran's nuclear program"; the deal is "strictly monitored" by international watchdogs; Iran is in compliance with the agreement; the agreement never expires; the deal "was never intended to solve all of our problems with Iran."

He added, "I believe that the decision to put the JCPOA at risk without any Iranian violation of the deal is a serious mistake."

Kerry, who has been publicly lobbying for US allies in recent weeks to salvage the agreement, issued his own statement condemning the withdrawal. "Today's announcement weakens our security, breaks America's word, isolates us from our European allies, puts Israel at greater risk, empowers Iran's hardliners, and reduces our global leverage to address Tehran's misbehavior while damaging the ability of future administrations to make international agreements," Kerry said. "No rhetoric is required. The facts speak for themselves. Instead of building on unprecedented non-proliferation verification measures, this decision risks throwing them away and dragging the world back to the brink we faced a few years ago."

Kerry added, "The extent of the damage will depend on what Europe can do to hold the nuclear agreement together, and it will depend on Iran's reaction. America should never have to outsource those stakes to any other country. This is not in America's interests. We should all hope the world can preserve the nuclear agreement."

The leaders of France, Britain and Germany quickly denounced Trump's decision.

Pompeo Vows 'Strongest Sanctions in the History of Iran'

DOA: Secretary of State, Mike Pompeo, vowed on Monday, the 21st of May, to levy an "unprecedented" level of sanctions on Iran after the US announced it was withdrawing from the 2015 nuclear accord.

In his first major foreign policy address since becoming chief diplomat, Pompeo laid out 12 pillars the US would demand from Iran for a new deal, even as he said a new agreement is "not the objective" of the Trump Administration.

Russia Conducted the World's Longest Surface-to-Air Missile Test

DOA: Russia has test-fired surface-to-air missile 50 miles farther than anyone has before, US intelligence sources revealed.

With little fanfare, Russia successfully used an S-500 surface-to-air missile system to hit a target 299 miles away, which is 50 miles farther than any known test, CNBC reported.

Moscow said the system can intercept hypersonic missiles, drones and stealth warplanes, like the F-22 and the F-35, and would allow it to destroy targets at a near-space range. The test used a modified version of the missile used in the S-300V4 surface-to-air system.

Russian President, Vladimir Putin, said earlier in May that he wanted to prepare the S-500 systems for mass production, giving Moscow the ability to engage multiple targets, states a news agency.

Regarding the US-North Korea Summit

DOA: On 16th May 2018, North Korea threatened to pull out of the proposed June 12 Summit with US. In an angry statement, North Korea's vice-foreign minister, Kim Kye Gwan, accused the US of making reckless statements and harboring sinister intentions. He pointed the finger squarely at US National Security Adviser, John Bolton. "We do not hide our feeling of repugnance toward him," Kim Kye Gwan said.

A few days earlier, Mr. Bolton had said North Korea could follow a "Libya model" of verifiable denuclearization. This alarmed Pyongyang, which watched Libya's Colonel Gaddafi give up his nuclear program only for him to be killed by Western-backed rebels a few years later.

Kim Kye Gwan said in his statement that this was "not an expression of intention to address the issue through dialogue".

"It is essentially a manifestation of awfully sinister moves to impose on our dignified state the destiny of Libya or Iraq, which had been collapsed due to yielding the whole of their countries to big powers."

"We do not hide our feeling of repugnance toward [Bolton]."

Mr. Kim also warns Mr. Trump that if he "follows in the footsteps of his predecessors"—refusing to engage with North Korea unless it gives up its nuclear weapons—"he will be recorded as a more tragic and unsuccessful president than his predecessors, far from his initial ambition to make unprecedented success".

On Thursday, the 24th of May, President Donald Trump canceled the scheduled June 12 summit in Singapore with North Korean leader, Kim Jong Un, after recent sparring between the two countries over the planned nuclear talks but later suggested it might still go ahead.

On 26th May, the leaders of North and South Korea met in the demilitarized border area between the two countries. The meeting was only the second between South Korea's Moon Jae In and the North's Kim Jong Un. It came as the two sides continued efforts to put a historic US-North Korea summit back on track.

Finally, on June 12, 2018, the summit between North Korea and the US actually took place in Singapore.

SK: They shook hands—tightly, of course—and exchanged pleasantries. At first, they met one-on-one, except for the interpreters, and later, with a larger group of officials from both sides, followed by a working lunch.

A joint statement was prepared and signed by both Trump and Kim. North Korea made a broad level commitment "to work toward complete denuclearization of the Korean Peninsula". But the statement was without specific details regarding the item-wise work breakdown schedule relating to the dismantling of the nuclear stockpiles, leave aside timelines for the same. The phrase 'denuclearization of the Korean Peninsula' was itself not clearly defined.

On his part, Trump, at a post-summit press conference later, surprised one and all by saying he would suspend the Joint US-South Korea war exercises and, in the course of time, withdraw the US forces from South Korea. In doing so, he would save a lot of money for the US. This was quite unexpected as he had earlier not consulted South Korean leader, Moon, about this or with his military establishment. But for Kim Jong Un, it was music to the ears.

All in all, Kim Jong Un can be considered to be the winner of this first round. He had been in the driver's seat all the time and made full use of having attained a position of strength with that entire nuclear arsenal at his disposal.

Perhaps Iran will get some inspiration from Kim and try to follow the same path.

But was the summit a success?

Sure, a failure of the summit could have led to a possible confrontation. But preventing such a failure was just a one-foot bar for a successful high jump. Avoiding failure of that kind can hardly be called a success. Considering the fanfare, media attention and the tremendous amount of significance given to this summit between Trump and Kim, it looked as if there was a major problem of the human civilization that was being attempted to resolve.

What exactly was this problem that was to be solved?

In my view, the problem was none other than 'TRUMP' and 'KIM'. The two guys who created the problem by abusing and threatening each other with nuclear strikes and bringing the Doomsday Emblematic Clock closer and closer toward midnight suddenly decided to shake hands and solve their own personal problem.

So what can I say other than this: At a broad level—relating to peace in the region—the picture looks somewhat better than what it was a few months back when 'fire and fury' were the words in fashion. Substantial credit for this should go to the South Korean President, Moon Jae In, who stage-managed the entire show exceptionally well. To some extent, credit should also go to Kim for realizing and understanding the 'information in the field' correctly and making suitable adjustments in his approach to the problem accordingly.

As for Donald Trump, he did nothing much except go with the flow, for which meager act he congratulated himself endlessly and bragged and bragged wherever he went.

Besides, it was too early to say to what extent—if any—the problem relating to the denuclearization of the Korean Peninsula was taken care of.

And what about Kim's human rights violations? I guess this was not in anybody's agenda, with the result that KIM would continue to oppress and depress, not forgetting to suppress his own people. There will be no change in this, it appears.

SEPTEMBER 2018

The Biggest Trade War in Economic History Begins

SK: That was the title of a blog in The South China Post.

The US of A has been relentlessly firing shots of tariffs of hundreds of billions of dollars on China, followed by similar retaliatory measures by China. Neither of them is showing any intention of backing down.

Tariff shots were also fired by America on several other main trading partners, including its allies in the post-war Atlantic trading alliance, such as Canada, Mexico, South Korea, Japan and Germany. Some time back, Trump called India a tariff king.

> *"Top of FormBottom of FormWhile a country may try to destroy another by targeting its economy rather*

than its military, history suggests that a full-blown trade war inevitably leads to a shoot-out between nations…." – The South China Post

At that stage, it appeared that if Trump remained POTUS for SOME MORE TIME, trade wars would escalate into WW3 and ultimately into a nuclear war.

Both world wars were preceded by trade wars.

As someone said, "If goods cannot cross frontiers, armies will." And as I say, "If armies cannot cross frontiers, nukes will."

UPDATE AS ON DECEMBER 2018

DOA: The midterm elections were held in the United States in the first week of November. The Democrats won the House but the Republicans retained the Senate majority. Commentators in Europe were mostly of the view that the result was not too bad for Donald Trump. Some even opined that he could win the 2020 elections and continue for another term. However, almost all commentators were of the view that Trump was not good for the world.

The murder of the Saudi Journalist, Jamal Khashoggi, at the Saudi Consulate in Istanbul, Turkey and the CIA's conclusion that the Saudi Crown Prince ordered the killing could possibly change the equations pertaining to the relations between Saudi Arabia and the US and other countries. The $110 billion arms deal between the US and

Saudi may be jeopardized, which is bound to upset Donald Trump's calculations.

Fact checking revealed that the arms deal is worth only $14.5 billion and not $110 billion, as proclaimed by Trump, and the number of US jobs effected is just about 10000 and nowhere near a million jobs as Trump had tweeted. However, he shows no signs of going back on his friendship and his deals with the Saudis. This could isolate the US and adversely affect its relations with its allies in Europe. At this stage, it is hazardous to predict what might be the final outcome.

On the North Korea front, there was no further reduction in tensile stress. The findings of a Washington think tank revealed that North Korea was possibly progressing with its ballistic missile program in 16 hidden bases. In the words of CNN's Amanpour, "This has knocked everyone sideways." There is no indication yet that North Korea intends to start denuclearization or that the US intends to curtail sanctions on NK. No further summit between the US and NK is planned in the current year. However, there is no provocative rhetoric from either side. In that respect, the tensile stress is substantially less than what it was during the days of 'fire and fury'. But as I said earlier, there is no further reduction in the stress levels since the June 12 summit.

SK: The Bulletin of Atomic Scientists had their Annual Dinner Meeting in Chicago on November 8th, 2018. I happened to be in their mailing list and was consequently invited to the meeting as a delegate. I could not make it, but I had a question to ask about the mathematical relation (if worked out) between the location of the needle of the emblematic clock and the probability of a nuclear attack taking place anywhere in the world in one calendar year. In short, how serious was 'two minutes to midnight' in comparison with, say, 'three minutes to midnight'.

I interacted via email with their Communication Director, Janice Sinclaire, to ask the question. She promptly responded while thanking me for my interest in the doomsday clock and explained that it was not a predictor of a nuclear attack, but instead was a metaphor for the end of humanity. She said that the time was set by taking into account a variety of factors, including human-caused climate change and disruptive technologies. She also posted many links to the background of the clock and how it worked. These articles were quite useful in helping me obtain a better overall understanding of the subject.

For the past 70 years—as revealed in the articles—the doomsday clock has served as a clarion call to all of us—scientists, policymakers, artists and ordinary citizens—to get engaged and help build a safer and healthier planet. The time for world leaders to address the looming nuclear danger and the continuing march of climate change are long past. The time for citizens of the world to demand such action is now.

A 'BOAS' article titled, *Will Disruptive Technology Cause Nuclear War?*, written by Mathew Kroenig and Bharath Gopalaswamy was quite an eye-opening analysis, showing how new technology might cause nuclear conflict:

by upending the existing balance of power among nuclear-armed states. This latter concern is more probable and dangerous and demands an immediate policy response.

For example, let us say that X, Y and Z are the three big powers on Earth (the US, China and Russia, not necessarily respectively). Now, consider the possibility: X decides to launch a sophisticated cyberattack against Y's nuclear command and control, essentially turning off Y's nuclear forces. Then X follows up with a massive strike with conventional cruise and hypersonic missiles to destroy Y's nuclear weapons. Finally, if any of Y's forces happen to survive, X can simply mop up its ragged retaliatory strike with advanced missile defenses. Y will be disarmed and X's nuclear weapons will still be sitting on the shelf, untouched. All this time, Z has been watching the proceedings. It can do the same to X that X did to Y.

In short, as Putin says, "Whoever leads in AI will rule the world."

So the solution lies not in preserving second-strike capabilities but in preserving prevailing power balances more broadly.

In the words of the authors of the article on disruptive technology, *"The consequences of Washington losing the race for technological superiority to its autocratic challengers just might mean nuclear Armageddon."*

In January 2019, the Bulletin of Atomic Scientists placed the location of the needle of the Doomsday Emblematic

Clock unchanged at two minutes to midnight, the closest since World War II.

[IT IS TEA TIME AT THE SEMINAR.

(For further reading about all the 'INFORMATION IN THE FIELD' from Einstein's Relativity up to January 2019 in comprehensive detail, refer to Bright Light In The Sky).

THE ACTORS THEN REASSEMBLE.]

AE: Ultimately, the realization should manifest itself that 'good sense must prevail'. The past cannot be changed. But the future is in our hands.

JW: Yes, absolutely.

EW: Can we continue with the story?

DOA: Sure.

THE YEAR 2019

DOA: As I said earlier, in January 2019, the Bulletin of Atomic Scientists placed the location of the needle of the Doomsday Emblematic Clock unchanged at two minutes to midnight—the closest since World War II.

As expected, events are happening at break-neck speed. 2019 can be considered as the year when architects of war—with the kind help of the Deep States of America and many other countries—are drawing plans for WWIII. Possible candidates—countries—that could be the theaters of war are Iran, Israel, Saudi Arabia, US, Russia, China, Syria, Turkey, Iraq, etc., not forgetting Pakistan and India.

The Military-Industrial Complex was in full control during the year.

AE: You mean the DEEP STATE?

DOA: Yes, the deep state of the US was in full control, as is always the case when Republicans are in power. Over the years, it has been seen that when the Democrats are in power, the direction is toward peace in the world. But when the Republicans are in power, the direction is toward conflicts and wars. The difference is that, in the latter case, the angle of deviation is much sharper than in the former case, with the result that the general inclination is toward WAR. Currently— since Donald Trump became POTUS—the angle of inclination is getting sharper and sharper, and it simply cannot be ignored. Now, it has a stage where the Republicans are simply unconcerned about the world's opinion on America. They seem to say to the world:

"WE ARE WHAT WE ARE. We make the rules, we break them whenever we want to, we control the world economy and we can cripple others with sanctions. We have the largest collection of nuclear warheads in the world; we can attack and eliminate whosoever we want. WE ARE REPUBLICANS!"

The combination of TRUMP, POMPEO and BOLTON remained dangerous for the world, particularly so for America itself.

The next target of the 'Trio' was IRAN.

SK:　　Time was running out to save IRAN.

CFT:　　There was a solid CASE AGAINST WAR ON IRAN.

As spelled out in the Indian newspaper, The Hindu:

"If the US goes to another war in a region still struggling to recover from its past interventions, it will be morally calamitous and strategically ludicrous. First, Iran does not deserve this treatment. The country signed an international agreement in 2015 to limit its nuclear program in return for sanctions relief. It fully complied with the deal until Tehran announced this month that it would suspend some commitments made under the deal in protest against US sanctions. It was Mr. Trump who violated the deal first by pulling the US out of it last year and re-imposing sanctions on Iran. In a better world, Iran's adherence to the agreement would have been appreciated and the country allowed to reap the promised benefits of the deal. Instead, the Trump Administration punished it. Second, if the US goes to war, it will be a unilateral military action. It won't get the approval of the United Nations Security Council as Russia and China remain steadfastly opposed to military action. Even the US's European allies, including the UK, which supported the Iraq war, remain committed to the nuclear deal. The US

might get the support of Saudi Arabia and Israel, but it is not certain whether even these countries would like to get dragged into a full-blown war. A unilateral military action would further weaken international institutions and create more fissures in the Atlantic alliance." – Stanly Johny

SK: I am thinking, though I hope I am wrong, that the war on Iran will likely turn nuclear and lead to a global chain reaction involving the big three (Russia, China and the US). The US might be the worst sufferer, apart from Iran, of course.

EW: On what basis do you make these predictions?

SK: Three possible reasons:

1.   A harassed and failed Trump may do something silly to divert attention from his impending 'EXIT'.

2.   The current nuclear stockpile available with the US is fast RETIRING and may not last beyond 2030, and so the requirement to use it and provide justification to manufacture more warheads for the future security of the US.

3.   As the war on Iran is completely unjust, it is bound to lead to the involvement of several nations, especially Russia and China, to come to the rescue of Iran, hence turning global. Except for Saudi Arabia and Israel, and maybe a few more nations, the rest of the world is with Iran.

LDV: But Donald Trump was supposed to counter the deep state. What made him change his mind?

EW: Somehow, I am not very clear about the deep state. It is very confusing to me.

LDV: So it is. I ask CFT to give us more info "through the looking glass…how the deep state comes to America".

EW: What do you mean by 'come to America'? Come from where?

LDV: From Turkey, I guess. Over to CFT.

CFT: *Peter Dale Scott was a professor of Literature at the University of California. He wrote the book, The War Conspiracy, in which he argued that the US intelligence community had helped drive Washington into intervening in Vietnam. His continued interest in the war's origins soon spawned a greater interest in the Kennedy assassination. In February 2008, Scott made his first appearance on Alex Jones's radio show, Infowars. By then, Alex Jones was just beginning to become a national phenomenon. Jones's contention that the 9/11 attacks were an "inside job" had already given rise to a "truther" movement aimed at exposing the role of the CIA, the Mossad and international industrialists (principally those associated with the Bilderberg Group) in the attack. Scott's findings connected immediately with this line of thinking. Thereafter he made further live appearances on*

Infowars and published articles on the show's website. Other contributors to Alex Jones's brand soon began to integrate the deep state into their own analysis of the Obama Administration and the US government at large.

By 2016, *Infowars* prophesized that Donald Trump was the man most likely to defeat the deep state, which one commentator likened to a "satanic alliance" made up of bankers, "corporatists" and members of America's military-industrial complex.

It should be said that scholars other than Peter Dale Scott had toyed with ideas similar to the deep state within the American context. Tufts University Professor Michael Glennon proffered the term "double government" as early as 2014 in analyzing the lingering national security institutions that spanned the Bush and Obama administrations. The continuities between Bush and Obama, he argued, demonstrated the country had "moved beyond a mere imperial presidency to a bifurcated system—a structure of double government—in which even the President now exercises little substantive control over the overall direction of US national security policy."

At this point, it is not likely that "double government" will evoke the same power and significance as the deep state. Since the spring of 2017, the deep state has become firmly entrenched within America's political diction as the principal expression associated with parallel sources of power or clandestine politics. Efforts to define its substance have since varied from sincerely earnest endeavors to acts of pure ridicule. In the last *year, the term has assumed an especially partisan connotation within the United States.*

At least four of President Trump's most noted supporters have published book-length accounts of the deep state's campaign to undermine his administration. Scott, meanwhile, has continued to write and give interviews on the subject, stating recently that he hopes both "Trump and the deep state will bring the other to behave more moderately".

EW: Who wants war?

DOA: Zarif, the Foreign Minister of Iran, said at a meeting last month that four Bs were perfidiously steering the United States toward war with Iran. These were Saudi Crown Prince, Mohammed *b*in Salman, United Arab Emirates Crown Prince and de facto ruler, Mohamed *b*in Zayed, Israeli Prime Minister, *B*enjamin Netanyahu, and White House National Security Adviser, John *B*olton. The first two, Sunni Arab royals, see Iran as a regional nemesis; the latter two have made no secret of their hostility to diplomacy with Tehran and their desire, instead, for regime change there.

EW: So it's the four Bs who are interested in war?

DOA: Plus the leaders of major corporations + defense contractors + some adventure seekers, etc.

EW: Does Trump want war?

DOA: Zarif stressed that he believed that these four men (the four Bs) were at odds with President Trump.

He would prefer to cut a new deal with the Islamic republic rather than try to squeeze it into submission.

SK: He will always look at it from a business angle. He would prefer to let other nations fight Iran and restrict America's involvement in manufacturing and supplying bombs.

JW: No one can predict what Trump is going to do tomorrow, which includes himself.

CFT: Yes, it was reported at the time by New York Times that *"acting defense secretary Patrick Shanahan presented an updated military plan that included the possible deployment of 120,000 US troops in the Middle East, which could theoretically form the logistical springboard for a ground invasion of Iran. Shanahan did so at the apparent request of Bolton, who not long before issued a video of himself announcing the arrival of a US carrier group in the region in response to supposed new threats from Iran and its militant proxies in Iraq, Yemen and elsewhere.*

The high-level review of the Pentagon's plans was presented during a meeting about broader Iran policy....It was held days after what the Trump Administration described, without evidence, as new intelligence indicating that Iran was mobilizing proxy groups in Iraq and Syria to attack American forces.

The following day, Trump scoffed at the report but didn't deny that he would entertain such a commitment.

'It's fake news, okay?' he told reporters. 'Now, would I do that? Absolutely. But we have not planned for that. Hopefully, we're not going to have to plan for that. And if we did that, we'd send a hell of a lot more troops than the 120,000 figure floated by the Times.'"

EW: What's the ground situation?

DOA: Some months ago, two oil tankers were attacked in the Gulf of Oman. Earlier, four oil tankers were attacked. 1500 troops were dispatched by the US to the Middle East. There is no clear evidence of who attacked the oil tankers. Washington, Germany, Saudi Arabia and even the UK are of the view that Iran is behind the attacks; this is being taken as a clear sign of Iran's hostile intent. 1000 additional troops are being dispatched to the Middle East as a prudent defensive measure by the Pentagon. Taken together, these deployments inevitably raise tensions but they are clearly not in any sense an assault force.

If direct conflict does break out between Washington and Tehran, it will most likely be a sporadic air and maritime battle, not a land campaign. Iran denies taking any part in the attacks. They blame the US squarely. The neighboring countries are also of the firm view that Iran is not involved. Some are of the opinion that, notwithstanding the mystery regarding who was responsible for the attacks, there is only one party who stands to benefit from the situation. And that is Iran. But despite Iran's denial, being blamed for these attacks suited it nicely.

CFT: *It's no surprise that Tehran has now announced an increase in the production of low-enriched uranium. Both moves help Iran's rulers turn a gap between the US and its most powerful allies in Europe into, well, a gulf.*

They also drive home the point that, whatever the US (and its allies in Saudi Arabia and Israel) may think, heavy economic pressure on Iran can have dangerous consequences. What worries Washington is attacks by the Iranian Revolutionary Guard Corps or Iran's proxies against US troops or facilities in the wider region. The US defense secretary is again insisting that Washington does not want conflict with Tehran, but tensions remain high and any miscalculation could lead to a serious escalation. Analysts now fear that the guardrails that once kept a perilous escalation at bay have fallen to the wayside.

DOA: In August 2019, the Indian government decided to scrap provisions of Article 370 that gave special status to Jammu and Kashmir, which led to a tense and dangerous situation in the region. The Muslim-majority state of Jammu and Kashmir enjoyed a unique status in predominant Hindu India for more than 70 years. But no more. Both houses of the Indian Parliament approved legislation to divide Kashmir into two "union territories" and allow non-Kashmiri Indians to move freely into the region, open businesses and buy land. Many Kashmiris feared the result would lead to a wave of migration that ends any hope of Kashmiri independence or autonomy.

Pakistan, which has fought three wars with India over Kashmir, reacted with rage, but it wasn't getting much support from its purported Muslim allies in the Persian Gulf region. At the UN also, Pakistan did not get support from any other country other than China.

There were some—including the Pakistan Prime Minister, Imran Khan—who tried to project an alarmist approach to the situation, which is far from the ground realities, and promoted violence in India including their leaders. Addressing a press conference after the UNSC meet concluded, an Indian representative said that Pakistan has been trying to mislead the world. China and Pakistan tried to pass their thought as the thought of the world community and that the view of China is not a global opinion. Imran Khan's rhetoric of a possible nuclear war with India is viewed with serious concern. Articles have been written, including one by the Bulletin of Atomic Scientists, describing how an India-Pakistan nuclear war might come to pass and what the local and global effects of such a war might be.

On September 14th, two predawn attacks were carried out on two major oil facilities in Saudi Arabia, knocking out more than half of the top global exporter's output. Yemen's <u>Houthi</u> rebels claimed responsibility but US Secretary of State, Mike Pompeo, swiftly accused <u>Iran</u>, which rejected the allegations.

Saudi Arabia, meanwhile, promised to "confront and deal with this terrorist aggression" while US President, <u>Donald Trump,</u> hinted at possible military action.

On 3rd October, Trump announced the withdrawal of US troops from Kurdish-held territory in Northern Syria. This opened up space for Turkey to attack the Kurds, who Turkey considered terrorists. Turkey's intent is to drive out the Kurdish presence along the Syrian-Turkish border and resettling Syrian refugees there. About 400 Kurdish fighters and 70 Kurdish civilians were killed in the Turkish offensive and more than 130000 were displaced.

Kurdish fighters of the Syrian democratic forces who helped—in a big way—the US counterterrorism efforts against ISIS in Syria are incensed at this atrocious betrayal by the US. This led to outrage from both Democrats and Republicans in the House and Senate. Republican Senators, Mitch McConnell and Lindsay Graham, two of Trump's strongest supporters, both admonished the president for his decision to withdraw troops from Syria. The Turkish offensive opens a wide lane for the resurgence of ISIS in Syria. ISIS detainees escape from the prisons in large numbers. This is likely to present a huge security risk for Europe. Foreign ministers of all 28 EU member states agree to stop selling arms to Turkey.

Pence and Pompeo then met Turkey's President, Erdogan, to broker a five-day ceasefire to allow the Kurds to leave. And then…

PUTIN MAKES A STRATEGIC MOVE ON THE CHESSBOARD.

He literally steps in to take center stage and meets Erdogan at the Black Sea town of Sochi, where they plan to carve out a 12000sq.km area (400km long x 30km wide) buffer zone across the Turkish border. The Kurds were to be driven out of this region called the 'safe zone'. Russian troops entered the region from where the US troops left. The zone will be jointly patrolled by the Russian and Turkish troops. Trump removed all sanctions on Turkey.

And so, Erdogan is happy, Putin is happy, Assad is happy, Trump is happy. They are the leaders of nations and their happiness counts, never mind if the common people everywhere are unhappy. Never mind if 400+ Kurd fighters and 70+ civilians had to lose their lives. Never mind if hundreds of thousands of people had to be displaced. Never mind if 1000+ ISIS prisoners escaped and are now free. Never mind if now there is a distinct threat of ISIS resurgence.

And so, it's a victory for Trump, as emphatically claimed by him. Never mind if it's a dramatic setback for US strategic and humanitarian priorities in Syria. Never mind if the US is now unable to secure the territorial defeat of ISIS and prevent its resurgence. Never mind if the US is now unable to provide a secure space with humanitarian relief for the diverse community of Christians, Kurds and others in the region who have looked to America for support. Never mind if the US has now lost its credibility.

I could go on and on to describe what has been going on in the last few months on this beautiful planet. Things are getting ugly.

Suffice to say, there's full chaos everywhere. The contamination of the field is in full flow. There is no break from the breaking news on CNN. And it's all bad.

Now, the war is on, and the original deep state (that of Turkey) has joined the other deep states of the world. Together, they are all set to create full-fledged chaos on the planet, not to mention creating war fronts in several regions.

And to top it all, there is an impeachment inquiry against President Donald Trump. Fiona Hill, Alexander Vindman, Marie Yovanovitch and many more have shown remarkable courage while standing against the rot in the White House. Come Christmas time, the world will know whether Trump will remain POTUS or not. The evidence against Trump is so damning that if he doesn't get impeached, it will show the American lawmakers and Trump's Republican allies, especially, in extremely poor light. Whichever way the result goes, it will have some effect on the world situation. An embarrassed POTUS could possibly do something silly.

SO WHERE WILL THE NEEDLE BE WHEN THE ATOMIC SCIENTISTS MEET AGAIN IN JANUARY 2020?

TWO MINUTES TO MIDNIGHT? ONE AND A HALF MINUTES TO MIDNIGHT? OR ONE MINUTE TO MIDNIGHT?

WHAT CAN I SAY OTHER THAN THIS: IT IS TIME TO ACT NOW!

That's it. I have placed all the cards on the table and all the information in the field from 1905 to November 2019. Now it's time for me to make my move. It's time for me to play the game of intuition, to make some assumptions, do some calculations and tell the world what lies ahead for us if good sense remains elusive.

EW: So what do we do now?

SK: We have done the differentiation part to understand the problem. Now we need to integrate to find the solution.

AE: Let's take a long walk. The campus at NIAS (National Institute of Advanced Studies), Bangalore, is really lovely for a long stroll in the park.

[They walk in groups of two. John Wheeler and Eugene Wigner are in one group. First off, they resume their argument on the information paradox as applicable in black holes.]

EW   *[jokingly]*: When all the information will eventually disappear in the black hole, what does it matter if, deep in the past, there was a war on Earth?

[JW looks at him sideways, in anger. They walk silently for some time. The topic then veers to simulation and the realization that simulation is the preferred choice over randomness. A simulation is necessary so that, as far as possible, everything happens in accordance with plans and designs to yield the desired results. In the case of the universe as a whole, the desired results are that life and consciousness exist and flourish in various parts of the universe. In the case of

human civilization, the desired results are peaceful coexistence, avoidance of conflicts and wars with compassionate, able and responsible leaders at the helm of every country and that randomness has little chance of coming in the way of the desired results.

All in all, it is to be ensured that men with an inadequate compassion and information index should have zero chance of becoming leaders of nations. The universe, they agree, is a quantum computer that computes its own behavior.]

JW: The processing of information keeps going on ad-infinitum. It is the information in the field that is responsible for what happens in reality. The complexities keep rising all the time.

EW: So what you are trying to say is that we must inject such information into the field that can prevent another war on Earth?

JW: Precisely.

[Albert Einstein walks with Erwin Schrodinger. Einstein talks about the historical development of religious thought from the religion of fear to the religion of morality. His view is that there is, in fact, a third stage of religious experiences that belongs to all of them, even though it is rarely found in its pure form.]

AE: I call it the 'cosmic religious feeling'. It is very difficult to elucidate this feeling to anyone who is entirely without it, especially as there is no anthropomorphic conception of God corresponding to it. The religious geniuses of all ages have been distinguished by this kind of religious feeling, which knows no dogma and no God conceived in man's image.

[Schrodinger talks about the unity of consciousness and the oneness of the mind.]

ES: One thing can be claimed in favor of the mystical teaching of the 'identity' of all minds with each other and with the supreme mind: The doctrine of identity can claim that it is clinched by the empirical fact that **'consciousness is never experienced in the plural, only in the singular'**. The mind is, by its very nature, a ***SINGULARE TANTUM.*** I should say the overall number of minds is just one. I venture to call it indestructible since it has a peculiar timetable, namely, the mind is always ***now.*** There is really no before or after for the mind. There is only a 'now' that includes memories and expectations. It could be that 'man's mind is a recent product of our planet's side', but if the first word (man) is taken out, I would not agree.

It would seem queer, not to say ridiculous, to think that the contemplating, conscious mind that alone reflects the becoming of the world should have made its appearance only at some time in the course of this 'becoming', should have appeared contingently, associated with a very special biological contraption which in itself quite obviously discharges the task of facilitating certain forms of life in maintaining themselves, thus favoring their preservation and propagation: forms of life that were late-comers and have been preceded by many others that maintained themselves without that particular contraption (a brain). Only a small fraction of them (if you count by species) have embarked on 'getting themselves a brain'. And before that happened, should it all have been a performance to empty stalls?

[Both agree in principle that the idea of 'unity of consciousness' and the 'oneness of the mind' was a 'Trump card' to converge all religions into one religion whose essence should be none other than 'to live in peaceful coexistence with one another', 'to live and let live', 'to take care of the environment around us', 'to find solace and peace of mind in prayer and meditation', etc. In this way, conflicts and wars can be eliminated altogether.

Leonardo da Vinci stays behind with the other three— DOA, CFT and SK—in the auditorium. He decides to help them edit the video recording of the day's proceedings. It would take some time. A message is sent to the scientists to keep walking and talking as long as they liked. The seminar would resume the next morning. LDV himself spends a long time thinking and planning what he would suggest the following day to prevent another war in the Middle East.]

LDV: I am thinking about the 'psychology of war'. There is no doubt that the common people of any nation don't want war. After all, it is the leaders of the country who determine the policy and it is always a simple matter to drag the people to their bidding. They just have to be told they're being attacked. It would be unpatriotic not to support their leaders.

But the present situation is unique. The war (proposed) on Iran—by the US—is entirely unjust. Neither the common people of Iran nor the USA want war. There is no inherent enmity between the two nations. The war is comprehensively being stage-managed by the deep state of the US. This should be made clear to the common people of the two nations by the news media, social media, the Pugwash Group, the Bulletin of Atomic Scientists, by books, etc.

And then the common people in both nations should come to the streets in millions and stage protest rallies against war. Hopefully, there will be no war. And if still there is war, all I can say is that the common people of America— the intelligent, compassionate and peace-loving ones—may find it difficult to bear the stigma of being led by rogue leaders who are engaging in an unjust and criminal war. It will make it even more difficult for them when they realize that they are paying for all this with their taxes.

SK:　And that is apart from the catastrophic consequences of the war, such as the number of people, including innocent civilians who may die, the number of US troops who may be killed, the economic consequences of the wars, the possible nuclear war and global chain reaction, not to mention, further contamination of the intelligent field.

End of Act One.

The next day, in that parallel universe, a video recording of Act One was shown on news channels worldwide, followed by a live performance of Act Two.

ACT 2

[Recorded classical music is in the air in the auditorium. The delegates arrive and settle down in their seats. On the second morning of the seminar, Handel's Organ Concertos greets them. All eight participants make themselves comfortable on chairs laid out in a semi-circle.

There is a new face—a ninth participant—who sits in the middle with four to his left and four to his right. This gentleman is none other than SV R-0, the revised version of Swami Vivekananda, who was urgently flown in from Interlaken, Switzerland, following a phone call made the previous evening by SK.

Also in the audience are several other scientists and important personalities, including world leaders, who were specially invited by Leonardo Da Vinci (RV), who will be called to the stage as and when required during the proceedings of the second day of the seminar.

The seminar is live on TV worldwide. Millions already saw the recording of yesterday's proceedings and got a relatively good idea of what was happening on their beautiful planet.

LDV is the moderator of the day's program.]

LDV: In rivers, the water that you touch is the last of what has passed and the first of that which comes; so with the present time, there is nothing we can do with the water that has passed. But we can control the water that is coming. There are three classes of people in the world: those who see, those who see when they are shown and those who do not see. Our job here is to show the right way to one and all and then hope for the best. Nature is the source of all true knowledge. She has her own logic, her own laws; she has no effect without cause or invention without necessity.

Our job is to determine and show the sequence of events that turn out to be the causes of such effects, which lead toward peace in the world and peaceful coexistence between the people of different nations, religions, cultures, etc., as well as between human beings and the environment around us. Many of us on this planet are in trouble and distress. But I love those who can smile despite the trouble, gain strength from distress and grow brave by reflection.

We have seen in the video that was shown to the public, the full information in the field and the extent to which the intelligent field has been contaminated on our planet. Now, it's one thing to make predictions of what calamities might happen if good sense remains elusive and quite another to show to the world what exactly is that good sense that can take us out of these predicaments. If the deep states of the nations have been able to stage-manage events to bring about wars and conflicts, why not the beautiful minds of the world stage-manage events to reverse the direction and bring about peace and peaceful coexistence.

With these thoughts in mind, I request the great minds assembled here to voice their views, and the great leaders of the world to listen to them and try to implement their suggestions. To begin with, I ask JOHN WHEELER and EUGENE WIGNER to please enlighten us with their views.

EW: Thank you, Leonardo. At the outset, let me call attention to the succession of layers of "laws of nature", each layer containing more general and more encompassing laws than the previous one and its discovery constituting a deeper penetration into the structure of the universe than the layers recognized before. However, it has to be said that all the laws of nature are conditional statements that permit a prediction of some future events on the basis of the knowledge of the present, except that some aspects of the present state of the world, in practice the overwhelming majority of the determinants of the present state of the world, are irrelevant from the point of view of the prediction.

JW: We will first understand how simple the universe is when we recognize how strange it is. The simplicity of that strangeness, Everest Summit, so well directs the eye that the feet can afford to toil up and down many a wrong mountain valley, certain stage by stage to reach someday that goal. Law without law. It is difficult to see what else than that can be the plan of physics. It is preposterous to think of the laws of physics as installed by a Swiss watchmaker to endure from everlasting to everlasting when we know that the laws must have come into being at some stage in the process of evolution.

Therefore, they could not have always been 100% accurate. That means that they are derivative, not primary…events beyond the law. Events so numerous and so uncoordinated that, flaunting their freedom from the formula, they yet fabricate firm form…The universe is a self-excited circuit. As it expands, cools, and develops, it gives rise to observer-participancy. Observer-participancy—via the mechanism of the delayed-choice experiment—in turn, gives what we call tangible reality to the universe…Of all the strange features of the universe, none are stranger than these: time is transcended, laws are mutable, and observer-participancy matters.

Observer-participancy means that the universe must have built into it from the beginning the potentiality for containing observers. Without observers, there is no existence. The activity of the observers in the remote future is foreshadowed in the remote past and guides the development of the universe throughout its history. The laws of physics evolve from initial chaos into the rigid structure of quantum mechanics because observers require a rigid structure for their operations and the laws are constrained by the requirement that the universe should provide a home for theoretical physicists.

On the one hand, in the domain of astronomy and cosmology, the anthropic principle constrains the structure of the universe. On the other hand, in the domain of atomic physics, the laws of quantum mechanics take explicitly into account the fact that atomic systems cannot be described independently of the 'INFORMATION' related to the experimental apparatus by which they are observed.

EW: Events so numerous and so uncoordinated that they can fabricate information that sometimes creates 'order' and sometimes contaminates the intelligent field sufficiently to create 'chaos'.

JW: Precisely.

EW: So it turns out there is no point in predicting what might happen in the future if good sense remains elusive. Rather, it is worthwhile to determine what 'good sense' is and how it can be implemented.

Yesterday, during a long, evening walk with John, we discussed, at considerable length, information as the nature of reality. The topic then veered to simulation and the realization that simulation is the preferred choice over randomness. A Simulation is necessary so that, as far as possible, everything happens in accordance with plans and designs to yield the desired results. In the case of the universe as a whole, the desired results are that life and consciousness should exist and flourish in various parts of the universe. In the case of human civilization, the desired results are peaceful coexistence, avoidance of conflicts and wars, compassionate, able and responsible leaders at the helm of every country and that randomness should have little chance of coming in the way of the desired results.

CFT: I think I have some valid objections to the physical simulation by intelligent designers:

1. Some computational substrate is required for the simulation to exist in and this computational substrate could easily be an abstract simulation in the realm of platonic forms.

2. It is not possible to create a simulation, except on a limited scale. A simulation of the universe, utilizing all the space and energy of that universe, would BE that universe and not a simulation.

EW: At the current level of knowledge, it is difficult to give a satisfactory reply to counter these objections without recourse to some metaphysics or teleology. But then the current level of knowledge is indeed insignificant compared to what it will be a few thousand years from now.

In about some hundred thousand years, we have become men from apes. It is reasonable to assume that after a similar time gap, or even less, we would become super minds. Then these problems of understanding simulation will not be insurmountable and what looks like teleology can be explained by science.

Now we have seen the extent to which the intelligent field on Earth has been contaminated and how close the Doomsday Emblematic Clock is to midnight. We have no choice other than reducing the contamination significantly and rewinding the clock toward safety. The problems are many, but they cannot be solved in isolation. The solution to all these problems should come together.

LDV: "The solution to all these problems should come together." I agree with that. Scientist Lee Smolin said something to the same effect in relation to the problems of science. Lee Smolin is here with us. I request him to come to the stage and enlighten us on this.

LS: Thank you, Leonardo.

There are only four problems that scientists have not been able to solve so far:

1.   How to combine quantum theory and general relativity to produce a single theory (of quantum gravity) that can claim to be a complete theory of matter.

2.   How to combine all the particles and forces in today's physics to give a theory as manifestations of a fundamental unity.

3.   To explain how the values of the free constants in the standard model of particle physics (the masses and lifetimes of the various elementary particles) are chosen in nature.

4.   To explain the existence and properties of dark matter and dark energy.

The above four problems will not be solved in isolation; the solution of these great problems will come together. A possible way forward is to give up the attempt to apply quantum theory to the universe as a whole and to regard quantum theory as the record of quantum information that one subsystem may have about another subsystem as a result of their mutual interaction. In this way, ideas from the study of quantum information may demonstrate how elementary particles may emerge from quantum space-time.

LDV: Thank you, Lee Smolin. I now request Seth Lloyd's take on the subject.

SL: In other words, the universe can be considered a quantum computer. One may ask the question, "But what does the universe compute?" My answer would be: It computes its own behavior. At first, the patterns it produces are simple, but as it processes more and more information, it produces more intricate and complex patterns—on the physical side, giving rise to galaxies, stars and planets, while on the human side, producing life, language, human beings, society and culture.

SK: They say that a classical computer cannot simulate a quantum mechanical system, so the universe, being quantum mechanical, cannot be considered a classical computer and can only be a quantum computer. My own idea is that all this happens in a field, and when sufficient information is accumulated in the field, it becomes an intelligent field in which the intelligence in the field keeps increasing all the time and this intelligence (like that of an infinite mind) is focused on creating biochemistries suitable for creating awareness and consciousness to understand itself. Hence, that portion of the computation, which the universe does, which is attributed to the intelligence of the intelligent field, is not completely in the domain of quantum computation. To some extent, it could even be called classical computation.

It could also be that the intelligent field is itself a product of simulation, which then simulates the universe. And it goes on and on, step by step, with trillions and trillions of intermediate steps, through trillions of years and countless eons of the universe. It is a universe created from nothing at all. It could be that we, human beings, are an intermediate step. This viewpoint also encapsulates the anthropic principle and explains what happens when a new eon of the universe is created. All the information is available in the field; all the constants of nature are already known to the intelligence in the field. It is just the 'switching on' that is needed. Whether to call it an intelligent field or an infinite mind or 'God' is, of course, just a matter of taste. The theists can call it God and the atheists should be happy to call it the intelligent field or the intelligent mind. The dispute should end.

CFT: The question that needs to be answered is this: At what stage did the computation begin that resulted in the creation of consciousness?

SK: Notwithstanding the fact that at the current level of our understanding, it is impossible to establish the number of eons that preceded the present eon of the universe and how simulation took place and under what mechanism the constants of nature could have been implanted in the system that 'switched on' the Big Bang. The fact remains that the operation was hugely successful in creating an eternal and everlasting universe (eon of) with life and consciousness evolving and flourishing in the galaxies.

All that is required now is to establish how the universe can make sense and what can be the philosophical model that ensures permanent consciousness for us all.

JW: Ultimately, it boils down to this: The processing of information keeps going on ad-infinitum. The complexities keep rising all the time.

CFT: So what you're trying to say is that we must inject such information into the field that can prevent another war on Earth.

JW: Precisely.

DOA: And what could that information be?

JW: That is the question.

LDV: Yes, that is the question. The present situation is unique. The war (proposed) on Iran by the US is entirely unjust. Neither the common people of Iran nor the USA want war. There is no inherent enmity between the two nations. The war is comprehensively being stage-managed by the deep state of the US. This should be made clear to the common people of the two countries by the news media, social media, the Pugwash Group, the Bulletin of Atomic Scientists, books, etc. And then the common people in both nations should come to the streets in large numbers and stage protest rallies against war. Hopefully, there will be no war then.

But of course, it is not so simple after all. What information exactly should be injected into the field to lead to such rallies? I expect some out-of-the-box ideas to emerge from this assemblage.

Yesterday, SK was heard talking on the phone, inviting and requesting someone to be one of the speakers today. I was wondering who it was and was pleasantly surprised to see Swami Vivekanand in our midst. I request him to please enlighten us with his ideas.

SV: Thank you, Leonardo. I completely agree with you. The common man anywhere in the world desires peace. The common man does not want war. The deep state of the US is predominantly at fault and is thriving on fanaticism and religious extremism in the Middle East. As such, the best option available is to consider fanaticism as a horrible disease and try to eliminate it altogether. Fanaticism, in turn, can be attributed to religious extremism.

Each religion brings out its own doctrines and insists upon them as being the only true ones. And not only does it do that, but it thinks that he who does not believe in them must go to some horrible place. Some will even draw the sword to compel others to believe as they do. This is not through wickedness but through a particular disease of the human brain called fanaticism. They are very sincere, these fanatics, the most sincere of human beings, but they are quite as irresponsible as other lunatics in the world. This disease of fanaticism is one of the most dangerous of all diseases. All the wickedness of human nature is roused by it. Anger is stirred up, nerves are strung high and human beings become like tigers.

It is a mistake to think that fanaticism can make for the progress of mankind. On the contrary, it is a retarding element creating hatred and anger and causing people to fight each other and making them unsympathetic. Sectarianism, bigotry and its horrible descendants have long possessed this beautiful Earth. They have filled the Earth with violence, drenched it often with human blood, destroyed civilizations and sent whole nations to despair. Emotions drag us down to the level of animals many times. Emotions have more connection with the senses than the faculty of reason; therefore, when principles are entirely lost sight of and emotions prevail, religions degenerate into fanaticism and sectarianism.

A man brings forth two or three doctrines and claims that his religion ought to satisfy all humanity. When a man stands and says, "My prophet is the only true prophet", he is not correct. He knows not the alpha of religion. Religion is neither talk nor theory nor intellectual consent. It is a realization in the heart of our hearts; it is touching God; it is feeling and realizing him. One man says that because his religion is the oldest, it is the best; another makes the same claim because his is the latest.

The history of the world teaches us that wherever there have been fanatical reforms, the only result has been that they have defeated their own ends.

If there is ever to be a universal religion, it must be one which will have no location in place or time, which will be infinite like the God it will preach. It will be a religion which will have no place for persecution or intolerance in its polity, which will recognize divinity in every man and woman and whose whole force will be created in aiding humanity to realize its own true divine nature. The power of religion, broadened and purified, is going to penetrate every part of human life. Therefore, religions will have to broaden. Religious ideas will have to become universal, vast and infinite.

In society, we see so many different natures. A thorough generalization of them is impossible but for our practical purpose, it is sufficient to have them characterized into four classes. First, there is the active man. His aim is to work—to build hospitals, do charitable deeds, make streets, to plan and to organize. Then there is the emotional man who loves the sublime and the beautiful to an excessive degree. He loves with his whole heart the great souls of all times, the prophets of religions and the incarnations of God on Earth. Then there is the mystic, whose mind wants to analyze his own self, to understand the workings of the human mind, what the forces are that are working inside and how to know, manipulate and obtain control over them. Then there is the philosopher who wants to weigh everything and use his intellect even beyond the possibilities of all human philosophy. So a religion to be equally acceptable to all minds must be equally philosophic, equally emotional, equally mystic and equally conducive to action.

[Applause from the audience.]

LDV: And of course, this combination will be the ideal of the nearest approach to a universal religion; even if there are differences of opinions about the nature of God or the form in which God exists, all religions must converge into a universal religion that teaches us that God is a mind. Thank you, Swami Vivekananda. Now, I request our friend, Erwin Schrodinger, to enlighten us on the 'oneness of the mind' or the 'unity of consciousness', which I believe is the central idea of universal religion.

ES: The reason why our sentient, percipient and thinking ego is met nowhere within our scientific world picture can easily be indicated in seven words: because it is indeed that world picture. It is identical to the whole and therefore cannot be contained in it as a part of it. But, of course, here we knock against the arithmetical paradox; there appears to be a great multitude of these conscious egos. The world, however, is only one. This comes from the fashion in which the world-concept produces itself. The several domains of 'private' consciousness partly overlap. The region common to all where they all overlap is the construct of the 'real world around us'. With all that, an uncomfortable feeling remains, prompting the following questions: Is my world really the same as yours? Is there one real world to be distinguished from its pictures introjected by way of perception into every one of us? And if so, are these pictures like unto the real world or is the latter, the world 'in itself', perhaps very different from the one we perceive?

Such questions are ingenious but, in my opinion, very apt to confuse the issue. They have no adequate answers. They all are or lead to antinomies, springing from the one source, which I call the arithmetical paradox; the many conscious egos from whose mental experiences the *one* world is concocted. There is only one possible solution to this paradox of numbers that answers these questions appropriately, namely the unification of minds or consciousnesses. There, multiplicity is only apparent. In truth, there is only one mind. This is the doctrine of the Upanishads.

Now, we do not wish to lose the logical precision that our scientific thought has reached and that is unparalleled anywhere at any epoch. Still, one thing can be claimed in favor of the mystical teaching of the 'identity' of all minds with each other and with the supreme mind: The doctrine of identity can claim that it is clinched by the empirical fact that **consciousness is never experienced in the plural, only in the singular**. Not only has none of us ever experienced more than one consciousness, but there is also no trace of circumstantial evidence of this ever happening anywhere in the world. If I say that there cannot be more than one consciousness in the same mind, this seems a blunt tautology—we are quite unable to imagine the contrary—i.e. the plurality of consciousnesses in one mind.

I find it utterly impossible to form an idea about either how, for example, my own conscious mind (that I feel to be one) should have originated by integration of the consciousnesses of the cells (or some of them) that form my body or how it should at every moment of life be, as it were, their resultant.

The fact remains that each of the component cells that go to make us up is an individual and a self-centered life is no mere phrase. It is not a mere convenience for descriptive purposes. The cell, as a component of the body, is not only a visibly demarcated unit-life centered on itself, it leads its own life; the cell is a unit-life and our life, which, in its turn, is a unitary life, consists entirely of the cells' lives.

Both the pathology of the brain and physiological investigations on sense perception speak unequivocally in favor of a regional separation of the sensorium into domains whose far-reaching independence is amazing because it would let us expect to find these regions associated with independent domains of the mind; but they are not. A particularly characteristic instance is the following. If you look at a distant landscape first in an ordinary way with both eyes open, then with the right-eye alone, shutting the left, then the other way round, you find no noticeable difference. The psychic visional space is in all three cases identically the same. Now, this might very well be due to the fact that from corresponding nerve ends on the retina the stimulus is transferred to the same center in the brain where 'the perception is manufactured'—just as for example, in my house the knob at the entrance door and the one in my wife's bedroom activate the same bell, situated above the kitchen door. This would be the easiest explanation, but it is wrong. To understand this, consider a thought experiment on the threshold frequency of flickering, a very interesting experiment.

Think of a miniature lighthouse set up in the laboratory and giving off a great many flashes per second, say 40 or 60 or 80 or 100. As you increase the frequency of flashes, the flickering disappears at a definite frequency, depending on the experimental details and the onlooker, whom we're supposed to watch with both eyes in an ordinary way, sees then a continuous light. Let this threshold frequency be 60 per second in given circumstances. Now in a second experiment, with nothing else changed, a suitable contraption allows only every second flash to reach the right-eye. Every other flash is to reach the left-eye so that every eye receives only 30 flashes per second.

If the stimuli were conducted to the same physiological center, this should make no difference. If I press the button before my entrance door, say every two seconds, and my wife does the same in her bedroom, but alternately with me, the kitchen bell will ring every second. However, in the second flicker experiment, it is not so. Thirty flashes to the right-eye plus alternating 30 flashes to the left are far from sufficient to remove the sensation of flickering; double the frequency is required for that, namely 60 to the right and 60 to the left if both eyes are open.

What then is the conclusion?

It is not a spatial conjunction of cerebral mechanism which combines the two reports. It is much as though the right-eye and left-eye images were seen each by one of two observers and the minds of the two observers were combined to a single mind. It is as though the right-eye and left-eye are elaborated singly and then psychically combined to one. It is as if each eye had a separate sensorium of considerable dignity proper to itself in which mental processes based on that eye were developed up to even full perceptual levels. Such would amount physiologically to a visual sub brain. There would be two such sub brains, one for the right-eye and one for the left-eye. The contemporaneity of action rather than structural union seems to provide their mental collaboration.

Thank you.

[Applause from the audience.]

Dr. Clifton Meador: I have a question about the flickering light thought experiment. Consider the two visual cortices: occipital and parietal lobes of the cerebral cortex.

The occipital visual cortex is at the back of the head. It receives visual images from the retina of the eye. The nerve pathways from the medial retina (closest to the nose) cross the back of the eye at the optic chiasm. Thus, the images from the left medial retina cross to the right occipital lobe and the images from the right medial retina cross to the left occipital lobe. The left medial retina thus sees objects laterally out in the left visual field; likewise, the right media retina sees objects laterally in the right visual field. The lateral retinal nerves both go back to the occipital lobe on the same side of the brain.

These lateral retinas "see objects" in the central visual fields (central vision). Thus, a destructive lesion to the occipital lobe, say on the right side of the brain, will cause complete blindness to the entire left visual field. The person, so blinded, will "see" nothing to the left of his nose. These lesions to the occipital lobe are quite rare but give an opportunity to study some details of vision. Now, take a person with a destroyed right occipital lobe and shine a point of light at him from the blind left visual field. Ask the person to point at the light source and he will do it with great accuracy with his hand, even though he cannot "see" it consciously.

These light images go to the opposite parietal visual lobe of the brain, located on the top and lateral sides of the brain. These visual cortices of the parietal lobe see form and shape and motions. These are all unconscious visions—not seen in the conscious mind. If we did not have these unconscious visual abilities, all sorts of objects and insects and whatever would fly into our eyes. Our conscious vision is too slow to care for our eyes by averting our heads. The parietal lobes "see" objects, even though the person may be blind from a destroyed occipital lobe.

I am not sure how this all fits with the flicker experiment but I thought this background would be helpful in our discussions.

ES: Good question and your analysis is perfect and makes it clear about the physical connection—in time and space—between the right side of the brain and the left visual field and between the left side of the brain and the right visual field. Now, how does all this fit with the flicker experiment? Consider the words of Charles Sherrington, "It is not the spatial conjunction of cerebral mechanism, which combines the two reports; it is as much as though the right-eye and the left-eye images were seen each by one of two observers, and the minds of the two observers were combined to a single mind, and so forth."

What I believe Sherrington is trying to say is that, even though there may be a physical connection in time and space, it is not this spatial conjunction (presumably this connection in time and space) which combines the two reports. I think we have to see it in the light of the nature of the thought experiment, which provides us with an initial condition that there is a suitable contraption which allows only every second flash to reach the right-eye and every other flash to reach the left-eye so that every eye receives only 30 flashes per second, which is not enough to remove the sensation of flickering.

So if there are two observers (each with both eyes open) and the same contraption is used, which allows only every second flash to reach one of them and every other flash to reach the other one, each observer will see only 30 flashes per second and the flickering sensation persists. Now, if the contraption is removed and there are 60 flashes per second, the flickering sensation goes and each observer sees a continuous light even if he chooses to close one of the two eyes. This means that there is a *mind* that makes the connection between the eyes of an observer and it is the same mind that makes the connection between the two observers, except that, physically, this connection between two observers does not materialize for the simple reason that the consciousness of each is in the singular.

SK: I guess there is a common denominator between Dr. Meador's analysis and the flickering light thought experiment; I call it an intelligent field, which we call the "mind". It designs and builds this physical connection. As Sherrington says, "Contemporaneity of action rather than structural union seems to provide their mental collaboration." Now, it is true that a single nerve cell inside us is never a miniature brain; it is just one out of trillions and trillions of them, each one, though aware in the singular, is just an insignificant part of us and we, in turn, are conscious in the singular.

However, our consciousness is the sum total of the awareness of these individual cells; when we consider a single-celled independent creature, such as paramecium, it looks as if this single cell is indeed a miniature brain, for it can swim toward food, retreat from danger and negotiate obstacles. This is curious, but it strengthens my viewpoint about the ever-present intelligent field and how a mind, when it encounters certain biochemistry, acquires a component of this intelligent field and gets awareness.

[At this stage, another gentleman from the audience—a certain revised version of Immanuel Kant—enters the conversation.]

IK: Now, since the notions of good and evil, as consequences of the a priori determination of the will, imply also a pure practical principle and, therefore, a causality of pure reason; hence, they do not originally refer to objects (so as to be, for instance, special modes of the synthetic unity of manifold of given intuitions of one consciousness) like the pure concepts of the understanding or categories of reason in its theoretic employment; on the contrary, they presuppose that objects are given; they are all modes (modi) of a single category, namely that of causality, the determining principle of which consists in the rational conception of a law which as a law of freedom, reason gives to itself, thereby a priori proving itself practical.

However, as the actions on the one side come under a law, which is not a physical law but a law of freedom, and consequently belong to the conduct of beings in the world of intelligence, yet on the other side as events in the world of sense they belong to phenomena; hence, the determinations of a practical reason are only possible in reference to the latter and, therefore in accordance with the categories of the understanding; not indeed with a view to any theoretic employment of it, i.e., to bring the manifold of (sensible) intuition under one consciousness a priori....But only to subject the manifold of desires to the unity of consciousness of a practical reason, giving it commands in the moral law, i.e., to a pure will a priori.

SK   *[to Albert Einstein]*: Sir, could you simplify that?

AE: I think the gist of what Immanuel Kant is saying is, "Before we make our judgment of whether something is 'good' or 'evil', we must ask ourselves under which law we are making the judgment…whether it is the law of freedom (of will)…or if it is a physical law (law of physics). The former from considerations of 'Pure Practical Reason' corresponds to the conduct of beings in the 'world of intelligence' and the latter from considerations of pure reason (theoretical) would mean that any act performed is in the world of sense, i.e., just a phenomena, i.e., merely the motion of atoms and molecules in accordance with the laws of causation."

[Another gentleman from the audience, the revised version of Amaury De Reincourt, then enters the scene.]

ADR: We should, however, not overlook the fact that logical thought and creative experience move in two contrary directions—one, according to the rational intellect, which, geared to act on the objective world of matter and partaking of its structure, descends toward it and turns its back on life; the other, moving in the same direction as life, involves the whole of consciousness with its intuitive component.

Kant thinks of intuition as being ***infra***-intellectual, whereas I think it is ***supra***-intellectual, overflowing and surrounding on all sides the narrow limits of the rational mind as the iris of the eye surrounds the pupil. This is the fundamental discovery of Eastern thought. The sense perceptions are superior to the physical body; the mind is superior to the senses, intuitive understanding is superior to the mind and above all, the self is superior to intuitive understanding.

LDV: Thank you, Schrodinger. So the 'unity of consciousness' and the 'oneness of the mind', can these be the Trump card ideas that can help unite religions? Now, I ask Einstein for his views on the unification of science and religion and his elaboration of the 'cosmic religious feeling' about which he wrote extensively in his book, *Ideas and Opinions*.

AE: Thank you, Leonardo.

Everything that the human race has done and thought is concerned with the satisfaction of deeply felt needs and the assuagement of pain. One has to keep this constantly in mind if one wishes to understand spiritual movements and their development. The development from a religion of fear to moral religion is a great step in people's lives. The truth is that all religions are a varying blend of both types, with this differentiation: that on the higher levels of social life, the religion of morality predominates.

Common to all these types is the anthropomorphic character of their conception of God. In general, only individuals of exceptional endowments and exceptionally high-minded communities rise to any considerable extent above this level. But there is a third stage of religious experience which belongs to all of them, even though it is rarely found in the pure form: I shall call it **cosmic religious feeling**. It is very difficult to elucidate this feeling to anyone who is entirely without it, especially as there is no anthropomorphic conception of God corresponding to it. The religious geniuses of all ages have been distinguished by the kind of religious feeling, which knows no dogma and no God conceived in man's image.

Question from the audience: But how can cosmic religious feeling be communicated from one person to another if it can give rise to no definite notion of a God and no theology?

AE: In my view, it is the most important function of art and science to awaken this feeling and keep it alive in those who are receptive to it.

We thus arrive at a conception of the relation of science to religion very different from the usual one. When one views the matter historically, one is inclined to look upon science and religion as irreconcilable antagonists and for a very obvious reason. The man who is thoroughly convinced of the universal operation of the law of causation cannot for a moment entertain the idea of a being who interferes in the course of events—provided, of course, that he takes the hypothesis of causality really seriously. He has no use for the religion of fear and equally little for social or moral religion.

A God who rewards and punishes is inconceivable to him for the simple reason that a man's actions are determined by necessity, external and internal. So in God's eyes, he cannot be responsible, any more than an inanimate object is responsible for the motions it undergoes. Nobody, certainly, will deny that the idea of the existence of an omnipotent, just and omnibenevolent personal God is able to accord man solace, help and guidance; also, by virtue of its simplicity, it is accessible to the most undeveloped mind.

But, on the other hand, there are decisive weaknesses attached to the idea itself, which have been painfully felt since the beginning of history. That is, if this being is omnipotent, then every occurrence—including every action, every human thought and every human feeling and aspiration—is also his work; how is it possible to think of holding men responsible for their deeds and thoughts before such an almighty Being? In giving out punishment and rewards, he would, to a certain extent, be passing judgment on himself. How can this be combined with the goodness and righteousness ascribed to him?.

Science has, therefore, been charged with undermining morality, but the charge is unjust. A man's ethical behavior should be based effectually on sympathy, education and social ties and needs; no religious basis is necessary. Man would indeed be in a poor way if he had to be restrained by fear of punishment and hope of reward after death.

Now, even though the realms of religion and science in themselves are clearly marked off from each other, nevertheless there exist between the two strong reciprocal relationships and dependencies. Though religion may be that which determines the goal, it has, nevertheless, learned from science, in the broadest sense, what means will contribute to the attainment of the goals it has set up. But science can only be created by those who are thoroughly imbued with the aspiration toward truth and understanding. This source of feeling, however, springs from the sphere of religion. To this, there also belongs the faith in the possibility that the regulations valid for the world of existence are rational, that is, comprehensible to reason. I cannot conceive of a genuine scientist without that profound faith. The situation may be expressed by an image: Science without religion is lame; religion without science is blind. THANK YOU!

[Applause from the audience.]

LDV: That was most enlightening. Thank you, Albert Einstein. So, in your own words, it boils down to faith in the possibility that the regulations valid for the world of existence are rational, rather than blind religious faith in the existence of an anthropomorphic God.

SK: Some people say it is a mistake to apply logic and rational thinking in the realm of faith, but I say it is an even bigger mistake to develop one's faith without applying logic and rational thinking.

LDV: And so, if we apply logic, rational thinking, not forgetting scientific reasoning, we come to the conclusion that the out-of-the-box idea that can unite science with religion and converge all religions into one religion is the 'unity of consciousness'.

ES: ONENESS OF THE MIND.

PAUL DAVIES *[From the audience]*: INFINITE MIND.

ES: ATMAN = BRAHMAN.

SK: WE ALL HAVE THE SAME MIND (The Six Words).

AE: COSMIC RELIGIOUS FEELING.

SK: THE TRAVELING COSMIC MIND.

ROGER PENROSE *[From the audience]*: PROTO-CONSCIOUSNESS FIELD.

SK: INTELLIGENT FIELD.

LDV: So we all agree that the mind and consciousness have a central place in the ultimate nature of reality.

JOHN C BELL *[From the audience]*: Never mind whether the said idea is not professionally useful to contemporary scientists.

AE: Or practically useful to build machines.

SK: But it can be philosophically useful to unite science with religion, to unite people, to unite cultures, to unite religions, to unite factions within religions, to end conflicts and wars including civil wars and so on.

EW: After all is said and done, what is that information that must be injected in the field to prevent conflicts and wars, including nuclear wars, and to help in the continuation of this extraordinary intelligent life on Earth.

AE: I suggest we arrive at a manifesto to be adopted and suggest the methodology for its implementation.

INTERACTIVE SESSION

LDV: So the manifesto could be something like this. Correct me where I am wrong.

I will first spell out the six points of the manifesto and it will be followed by an interactive session where each topic of the manifesto can be discussed and deliberated and a methodology arrived at on how to implement the manifesto.

[Enter SH-R0 (the revised version of Sherlock Holmes) from the front row of the audience.]

SH: There need be only one point manifesto: Investigate the deep state. There is enough evidence against the deep state. Fool proof evidence. Evidence not of what actually happened on 9//11 but rather of what 'did not happen' or could not have happened without violating Newton's third law. The evidence lies in the statement: "Newton's third law cannot be violated. It was never violated in the past; it will never be violated in the future."

[IN-R0 (the revised version of the great Isaac Newton) speaks up from the audience.]

IN: Absolutely.

ES: Be careful, Sherlock Holmes. This matter needs to be dealt with subtly. It should not lead toward the cardiac arrest of the human race.

LDV: Truth, at last, cannot be hidden. Dissimulation is of no avail. Dissimulation is to no purpose before so great a judge. Falsehood puts on a mask. Nothing is hidden under the sun. If we find from our own experience that something is a fact and it contradicts what some authority has written down, then we must abandon the authority and base our reasoning on our own findings.

ES: Yes, I do believe that the present understanding of what happened needs to be altered, perhaps by a bit of blood transfusion. But that will not be easy; we must beware of blunders. Blood transfusion always needs great precaution to prevent blood clotting. So as I said before, the matter needs to be dealt with subtly.

LDV: Yes. It should be realized that the deep state is not just an American issue. Many DEEP STATES in the world need to be dealt with such as. The deep state of corruption at high places spread across many countries, including India. There is the deep state of racism, the deep state of white supremacism, the deep state of religious extremism, the deep state of Islamic fundamentalism, the deep state of extreme violence and murder to grab resources and so on. Truly, man is the king of beasts for his brutality exceeds them. We live by the death of others. We are a burial place.

ES: It is a universal phenomenon, a natural phenomenon. Nature has no reverence toward life. Nature treats life as if it were the most valueless thing in the world. Produced million-fold, it is for the greatest part rapidly annihilated or cast as prey before other life to feed it. This precisely is the master-method of producing ever-new forms of life. 'Thou shalt not torture, thou shalt not inflict pain.' Nature is ignorant of this commandment. Its creatures depend upon racking each other in everlasting strife.

The universe of energy is, we are told, running down. It tends fatally toward equilibrium, which shall be final. An equilibrium in which life cannot exist. Yet life is being evolved without pause. Our planet in its surround has evolved it and is evolving it. And with it, evolves the mind. If the mind is not an energy system, how will the running down of the universe affect it? Can it go unscathed? Always, so far as we know, the finite mind is attached to a running energy system.

When that energy system ceases to run what of the mind which runs with it? Will the universe which elaborated and is elaborating the finite mind then let it perish? Such considerations are in some way disconcerting. The thing that bewilders us is the curious double role that the conscious mind acquires. On the one hand, it is the stage and the only stage on which this whole world-process takes place. On the other hand, we gather the impression, maybe the deceptive impression, that within this world-bustle the conscious mind is tied up with certain very particular organs (brains), which, while doubtless, the most interesting contraption in animal and plant physiology are yet not unique, not *sui generis*; for like so many others, they serve after all only to maintain the lives of their owners, and it is only to this that they owe they're having been elaborated in the process of speciation by natural selection.

EH   *[Revised cosmologist, Ed Harrison, from the audience]*: But in case of the human mind, as it evolves toward an intelligent human being, after a span of time, natural selection must operate on a different scale altogether. Indeed, we are the outcome of natural selection and the operation of this law can be attributed to the fitness of the human body. When a civilization gains control of its environment, the evolutionary game must change and new rules determine what is fit and unfit. Natural selection must operate differently. According to the new law, "intelligent life-forms that are destructively aggressive cannot—or should not—control the environment". This law must operate conceivably in two modes; the first is unconscious and automatic and the second is conscious and deliberate. There is every hope that the evolutionary process—with the kind help of the great scientists—will lead toward 'super-intelligent human beings' in the future in total control of the environment.

ES: So while there are various deep states attributed to human beings, the unity of consciousness implies that no individual human being is to be blamed, least of all individual human beings from America nor any nation is to be blamed. A nation is just a geographical area, and Americans are by and large intelligent and compassionate human beings and so are people from other countries. It is the interactions of the world that make people what they are, and how many of them become victims of time. It is the deep state phenomenon that needs to be controlled.

AE: In essence, America is predominantly a GOOD STATE, and now is the time for the good state of America to first control and then eliminate the deep state of America. And there is no need for the 9/11 story to be a stigma for the American public. It is best forgotten as an aberration of the past. But the public must be aware of the story and be conscious and aware that the deep state must not be permitted to stage-manage another war in the Middle East or elsewhere by random manipulation of events here and there.

[The audience rises and a standing ovation follows.]

LDV: Very well said, Einstein. You first saved the human race by writing a certain letter to President Roosevelt, which ultimately prevented the Germans from making the first use of the atomic bomb, and now you have made a strong statement that should prevent the deep state from stage-managing any more conflicts or wars.

SK: Let us attribute this worldwide deep state phenomenon to the existence of an 'unintelligent field' out there.

EW: So there is an intelligent field and an unintelligent field and there is a war between the two.

SK: And the unintelligent field is leading.

AE: We'll see about that. Don't worry.

JW: As they say, "Have no fear, Einstein is here."

EW: So what do we do?

AE: Proceed with the manifesto.

LDV: Here we go:

1. The United Nations secretary-general should invite the United States and all the other signatories—the UK, France, Germany, Russia and China—of the JCPOA for an urgent meeting with a constructive attempt to reach an agreement, comprehensively reduce tensions and take full control of the situation and absolutely avoid any military confrontation from any side. Illegal economic sanctions re-imposed against Iran must be lifted. After a thorough discussion among the participants, a revised nuclear deal, which is acceptable to all stakeholders, must be adopted and implemented. Needless to say that all the participants who arrive at the meeting should have a neutral perspective and should

> not consider themselves members of this or that nation or this or that party. Rather, experts should address all problems in a scientific manner and from a human perspective and the common man's perspective and not allow egoist leaders of any nation to have any say in the matter.

CFT: The world powers (minus the United States) believe that the world's most comprehensive nuclear agreement, namely the JCPOA, should be revived. By all official accounts, the JCPOA was working very well in achieving one crucial objective: preventing Iran from obtaining a nuclear weapon. President Trump has <u>repeatedly said</u> that he is looking to achieve the same objective, that is, "for Iran to remain a non-nuclear state." The JCPOA is the most robust and comprehensive international mechanism that can prevent Iran–or any other country for that matter—to acquire a nuclear weapon. Therefore, if the United States is serious about non-proliferation, it should work with Iran, the regional and the world powers to regionalize the principles of the JCPOA, which would ensure zero nuclear bombs in Iran and the region. A de-nuclearized Middle East is the only sustainable solution, and the JCPOA has created a new foundation to achieve this goal.

LDV: In continuation:

1. The common people of Iran should come out to the streets in their thousands, in peaceful

protest rallies across the country, and ask the question to the common people of the US: "Do you really want to attack us?" The common people of the US should come out to the streets in their thousands, in peaceful protest rallies across the country, and tell the common people of Iran: "No, we don't want war with Iran."

2.   Dialogue should begin straightway between the leaders of Iran and the leaders of Saudi Arabia. As indicated in the Article 5 of UN Security Council Resolution 598, to contain the escalating tensions in the Persian Gulf and to secure a steady supply of energy to the world market while preventing any military confrontation, Iran, the Arab countries around the Persian Gulf and the five permanent members of the Security Council will need to have direct contact. A sustainable peace and security arrangement in the region will necessarily require the stakeholders to hold *direct* talks. In this respect, direct contact between Iran and Saudi Arabia is all the more necessary.

CFT: Iran is prepared for dialogue if Saudi Arabia is also ready. Tensions have spiked between Iran and Saudi Arabia, arch-rivals for predominance in the Middle East since Riyadh accused the Islamic republic of carrying out attacks that damaged six oil tankers in the Gulf, an allegation Tehran has denied. The attacks on the oil tankers came as the United States,

Saudi Arabia's major big-power ally, toughened sanctions on Iran in a bid to force it into negotiations on stricter limits to its nuclear activity and curbs on its ballistic missile program. Iranian Foreign Minister Javid Zarif said some time back, "If Saudi Arabia is ready for dialogue, we are always ready for dialogue. We have never closed the door to dialogue with our neighbors and we will never close the door to dialogue with our neighbors."

SK: However, as we have all agreed, the solution of all the problems must come together, and in this respect, I have to say that dialogue between Iran and Saudi Arabia is unlikely to materialize unless there is a resolution of conflicts between the Shias and Sunnis, across the world. In my view, this is perhaps one of the biggest conflicts on the planet and possibly one of the easiest to resolve. In this respect, it shows the intelligence of humans in extremely poor light. In other words, the UNINTELLIGENT FIELD is in control over the situation.

A statistical analysis will show that the dispute between Shias and Sunnis is non-existent in non-Muslim countries. It is also more or less non-existent in Muslim-majority nations, which are either predominantly Sunnis, such as Saudi Arabia, or predominantly Shias, such as Iran. However, the problem does exist significantly in Muslim-majority nations where the ratio of Shia: Sunnis lies within 0.25 and 4.0, for example, Iraq and Syria, where this dispute is rampant and is the root cause of the frequent civil wars.

There is no doubt that there exists a massive divide between the various factions of Muslims (in particular the dispute between Sunnis and Shias, also known as Shiites). The divide began after the death of the prophet Mohammad. His followers could not agree on who was his successor. Those who considered the bloodline successor to be Ali (his cousin and son-in-law) were called Shiites and those who chose Abu Bakr (his adviser) as the successor were called Sunnis. This divide is difficult to understand, considering the fact that centuries have passed since Mohammed's death, as well as the death of his successors. Why is there a need to choose a successor when Mohammad himself can be chosen as he is the common denominator? I ask the following questions: Why do we need a successor? Do Buddhists want to know who Buddha's successor was? Do Christians want to know who Christ's successor was?

There appear to be enormously wide variations in the ideologies and beliefs of the people in nearly every aspect of life, not just religion. Over the years, the split between factions widened appreciably, based on divisions due to different interpretations of the sacred texts, the role of mysticism and whether the old tenets of faith should be updated or reformed. The common people of both sects are no different from each other. It's only the leaders who exploit them for political ends and to obtain support for their own causes, regardless of whether they are good causes.

Hence, the religious leaders of both the factions must assemble in a conference and resolve the conflict. Needless to say, all the participants who arrive at the meeting should have a neutral perspective and should not consider themselves to be members of this or that faction. Instead, they should see themselves as experts and address all problems in a scientific manner and from a human perspective and the common man's perspective, not allowing egoist leaders of any particular faction have any say in the matter.

However, the conflict between Shias and Sunnis cannot be an isolated problem and needs to be addressed in conjunction with the resolution of conflicts between different religions of the world, especially between the Muslim faith and other beliefs of the world. The parts of the religious documents that relate to the intolerance of the so-called "nonbelievers" surely need to be reformed. I ask the following questions: Is there a nonbeliever? What does he or she look like? Is he or she wearing a T-shirt that reads, 'I am a nonbeliever'?

In essence, we cannot decide (or calculate) what we are, believers or nonbelievers, unless we can define what 'God' is. What is the initial condition, or the definition, of God based on that we can calculate and determine whether we are believers or nonbelievers? Now, if we follow the dictionary meaning of God, which defines God as a 'super human being' who controls nature, it turns out that we are all nonbelievers for the simple reason that an anthropomorphic God—as very nicely explained by Einstein—(one who has physical function, one who is made up of atoms and molecules, one who is sitting somewhere in the Andromeda Galaxy and keeping a comprehensive track of the deeds of all the living creatures of the universe and then who rewards and punishes accordingly) cannot exist without violating the laws of science created by him.

On the other hand, if we define God as an 'intelligent field' that controls nature, then we are all believers. However, it is to be understood that the quantum of intelligence or stupidity is a measure of the information in the field. Such an intelligent field, or God, is unlikely to come to our rescue if we are hell-bent on fighting wars. So it turns out that we are all believers and thus not in dispute with each other. No harm will be done if our religious documents are reformed to incorporate this truth.

LDV: In continuation:

1. There is an urgent need for a synthesis of science and religion in education. Science and religion must converge, which would then result in the convergence of all religions into a single religion.

SR (Swami Rangananthananda) *[from the audience]*: Education has to enable all students to achieve at least a fraction of the synthesis of East and West, spirituality of science, contemplation and action. It is the science of spirituality, the para vidya, the supreme science, that fosters in man ethical, aesthetic and spiritual values, including the moral values associated with pure science. The harmony of all these values and the intrinsic harmony between science and religion always upheld in Vedanta became revealed in our time in the deep spiritual kinship between Swami Vivekananda, the representative of aparavidya, and Shri Ramakrishna, the full embodiment of para—vidya. All such values emerge from out of the depths of the human spirit at a certain stage of human evolution and after the achievement of some measure of mastery of the environment by him; they do not emerge from physical nature himself. It is folly, therefore, to believe or to expect that they will automatically result from industry or from technological manipulations of physical nature and from the wealth resulting from such achievements.

BR (The revised version of Bertrand Russell): The machine as an object of adoration is a modern form of Satan. Its worship is modern diabolism. Whatever else may be mechanical, values are not and this is something no political philosopher must forget.

MW (Michael Welker): The resurrected Jesus Christ is not the resuscitated pre-Easter Jesus of Nazareth. The entirety of Jesus's life, his charisma and his power are present and efficacious in the resurrected and exulted one. The complete fullness of his person and his life is now present 'in spirit and faith', but this is hard to comprehend to naturalistic and scientific thought.

SK: The subject needs to be viewed in the context of the information theory. People order their lives based on their beliefs, which, in turn, are based on the information accessible to them. This, in turn, is based on the past interactions of the rest of the world on them, which has made them what they are. There is no doubt that the presence of such information in the field that gives solace and peace of mind in prayer and in the knowledge of Jesus's presence (in whatever form one can imagine) is very much helpful to mankind. However, when it is a question of "talking science" and discussing the subject in the context of its correlation with the information theory, we must ask the question: is resurrection a possibility? Why is it assumed that the answer provided to this question by a naturalist or a scientist will be different from that provided by a theologian, particularly in the light of the fact that the information—the data that constitutes the input to perform their analysis—available to all of them is the same in all respects, not to mention that all three of them are made up of the same atoms and molecules? Indeed, we must follow the teachings of the great religious leaders of the past, but there should be no reason to believe the events of rising from the dead, walking on water, or the carrying of a mountain on a finger.

On the other hand, it is to be realized that the presence of information on religions of the world, including that on mythology and religious philosophy, which leads people to go to the churches, temples and masjids, etc., or to perform rituals that provide solemnity to occasions such as marriages, festivals, etc., has over the years given immense happiness, solace and peace of mind to the people of the world and there is no reason to believe why they should not continue to do so. However, it is also to be realized that the presence of certain information in the religious doctrines that permit intolerance and jihad against other religions is full of self-endangerment and destructive potentials and has, over the years, caused religious extremism, conflicts and wars. There is no reason to believe why these doctrines should not be reformed.

All in all, when we talk science, the nature of reality is just information—the information in the intelligent field or the infinite mind. We may call this intelligent field or infinite mind our 'God', but this God is just a computer. No doubt it is intelligent; it gives us everlasting consciousness (everlasting in the sense that we are unconscious of our "unconscious tenures", so they pass quickly), it designs our bodies and their capacities to grow, and above all, it designs the laws of the universe with precisely calculated mathematical constants. However, this intelligence in the field is limited to the sum total of information acquired and processed through time. The quantum of intelligence is, of course, powerful enough to sustain the universe, which is impressive, but whether or not we can call it "divine" is a matter of taste. We must take into consideration the fact that many times, life can only live at the expense of other life and that most living creatures kill each other in everlasting strife.

LDV: In continuation:

1. Conflicts between nations and within nations must be resolved without any further delay.

AE: Scientific and analytical approaches would be required to resolve conflicts in the world in a way that is acceptable to all stakeholders. To explain the methodology, let us analyze one such conflict in comprehensive detail and arrive at a possible resolution.

LDV: Ok, consider the conflict between India and Pakistan. First off, let SK provide all the inputs he is aware of.

SK: It is to be noted that if a war breaks out between the two countries, it will have to be fought under a nuclear overhang. There is no doubt whatsoever that the presence of nuclear weapons has substantially changed the way war will be fought by these two nuclear adversaries.

In principle, there exists no conflict between the common people of the two nations. Hindus and Muslims have lived together for centuries; they look alike, they speak the same language, they sing the same songs, they watch the same movies, they have the same passion for cricket. There is no denying that the common people of the two countries would like to live in friendship and peaceful coexistence with each other. But this is denied to them by the armies of the two nations, in particular, Pakistan's army.

AE: 'The deep state of Pakistan'. Just as the deep state of the US stage-manages the conflicts in the world so as to remain in perpetual control to ensure business as usual for its Military-Industrial Complex, in the same way, the deep state of Pakistan, viz its military with the kind help of all the terrorist organizations under its control, stage-manages the continuation of the conflict against India to retain its importance as well as its financial health with complete disregard to the development of the nation.

SK: India and Pakistan indeed have some misunderstandings. There have been wars between them. There are complexities involved, such as that of Kashmir. These are not insurmountable and if left alone, they can be resolved, provided there is no interference by other countries. They are not impossible, provided also that the Pakistani army is under control of its civilian leadership that wants to "live and let live" with its Indian counterpart. The trouble is that neither of these provisions is forthcoming. The Pakistani army is in total control over policies concerning national security, particularly with respect to its enmity with India. I doubt if this enmity with India (of the Pakistani army, not the common people) will be reduced even if the Kashmir issue is resolved.

LDV: Nevertheless, that the Kashmir issue must be resolved is an important step toward the resolution of conflicts between Pakistan and India. The recent decision of the Indian Government to scrap provisions of Article 370 that gave special status to Jammu and Kashmir has apparently led to a situation in the region, which I think is tense and dangerous. How do we address the problem from a neutral perspective, in a way that is acceptable to the common people of Pakistan and

India, and above all to the common people of Jammu and Kashmir? I suggest CFT come forward with his views after taking into account the information relating to ground realities in the aftermath of the above decision by the Indian government, as well as after understanding the plight and suffering of the People of Kashmir during the last seven decades.

CFT: The Muslim-majority state of Jammu and Kashmir enjoyed a unique status in a predominantly Hindu India for more than 70 years. But no more. Both houses of the Indian Parliament have approved legislation to divide Kashmir into two "union territories" and allow non-Kashmiri Indians to move freely into the region, open businesses and buy land.

Many Kashmiris fear the result will be a wave of migration that ends any hope of Kashmiri independence or autonomy. Pakistan, which has fought three wars with India over Kashmir, reacted with rage, but it isn't getting much support from its purported Muslim allies in the Persian Gulf region. The entire Gulf region is substantially involved in business with India in a big way. Recently, Saudi Aramco announced a $15 billion investment in an Indian oil company. Pretty soon, Prime Minister Narendra Modi will travel to the United Arab Emirates to receive the country's highest civilian honor. From the U.A.E., he will travel to Bahrain on the first-ever visit to that country by a sitting Indian prime minister.

At the UN also, Pakistan did not get support from any other country other than China. After a certain closed-door meeting at the UNSC, China addressed a press conference on India's decision on Kashmir and asserted that the situation in J&K is "serious and dangerous".

China also said that India has "violated the bilateral agreement to keep peace in the border areas" by the constitutional amendment.

Indian representative, Syed Akbaruddin, defended India's decision, saying it was an internal matter of India. *"India remains committed to ensure that the situation in J&K remains calm and peaceful," he said. "These have no external ramifications, the recent decisions taken by the Govt of India and our legislative bodies are intended to ensure that good governance is promoted, social-economic development is enhanced for our people in Jammu and Kashmir and Ladakh," he said. Slamming Pakistan for interfering in the internal matters of India, Syed Akbaruddin said, "I have been a member of many delegations to Islamabad. There are normal ways of dealing but no democracy will acknowledge if you use terror to push your goals. Stop terror to start talks."*

Some tried to project an alarmist approach to the situation, which is far from ground realities, and promoted violence in India, including by their leaders. Addressing a press conference after the UNSC meet concluded, the Indian representative said that Pakistan has been trying to mislead the world. China and Pakistan tried to pass their thought as the thought of the world community, that the view of China is not a global opinion.

"History knows that the last agreement we signed in 1972, we adhere to that, but Pakistan also needs to follow that. We can go back in history. Every new agreement overtakes the past. We have already extended our friendship according to the Shimla agreement and we are committed to that." – Syed Akbaruddin

Other views: *"Civil libertarians and human rights activists in India and around the world have condemned the crackdown in Kashmir, but a recent opinion poll found 57% of Indians wanted Kashmir to lose its special status. Sixty-five percent said they thought Mr. Modi could solve the Kashmir problem in five years. I heard worries but few regrets from well-connected Indians in government, business and the academy. People told me that for decades, India has been lavishing money on Kashmir, but the money has gone nowhere. The Kashmiri economy is a disaster, the radicalization of unemployed and underemployed young people continues to worsen, and Pakistan has no interest in helping to stabilize the situation. Yes, I heard from many Indians, the new policy is risky and could set off another round of violence, but what are the alternatives?" – Walter Russell Mead (Journalist)*

LDV: Your views, Charley, from a neutral perspective—acceptable to all stakeholders—and toward resolution of the conflict.

CFT: I agree with Einstein that the deep state of Pakistan, viz its military, with the kind help of all the terrorist organizations under its control, stage-manages the continuation of the conflict with India. In this respect, the deep states of the world need to be taken care of by appropriate means. Intelligence must conquer the 'unintelligence'. I guess Leonardo will speak on the subject. But I do believe the Indian government's action to counter the deep state of Pakistan (The Pak Army – Terrorists Nexus) was sort of a knee jerk reaction. It could have been discussed with the Pakistan Civilian Leadership in a congenial atmosphere.

But of course, this was never forthcoming. It may be noted that over the years, there have been innumerable attempts made by the leaders of Pakistan and India to come to the negotiating table, but on each occasion, it was thwarted by the deep state with the help of the terrorists. And now the dialogue must still take place, but in a congenial atmosphere with intent to solve the problem, from a human being perspective and not from the perspective of this or that nation or this or that religion or this or that culture. Preference must be given to the well-being of the common people of Kashmir and for the overall development of the region. As Einstein has suggested, no religious basis is necessary.

AS (The revised version of the scientist, Abdus Salam):
Yes, no religious basis is necessary. And if at all religion is to be considered, it should be limited to the essence of religion. And just as it is desirable to comprehend the complexity of nature in terms of as few elementary concepts as possible, in the same way, the essence of religion can be limited to as few

principles as necessary, such as 'to live in peaceful existence with all', 'to live and let live', 'to find solace and peace of mind in prayer and meditation', 'to take care of the environment around us' and, above all, 'to respect, and not violate, the established principles of science'. Scientific thought and its creation is the common and shared heritage of mankind.

LDV: In continuation:

1. **INTELLIGENCE MUST CONQUER UNINTELLIGENCE**

Ultimately, it boils down to the requirement that intelligence must conquer unintelligence. Further, it must be realized that time is running out for 'I' to conquer 'U'. A victory for 'U' would mean the end of the world for the human race.

AE: Before we start analyzing and finding ways for 'I' to conquer 'U', it's better to understand the current status of the fight between the two. Who is leading now and where are we headed toward? What exactly is in store for us?

[Multiple voices are heard from the audience. Several hands are raised Stephen Hawking (the RVO) speaks first.]

SH: 'U' has a significant lead over 'I'. Randomness is extremely widespread. The deep states of the world are in control. They can stage-manage events by arranging frequent 'miscalculations' and leaving it to 'randomness' to retake charge. In this way, 'U' will always be in the lead. I may sound pessimistic but in my view, 200 years is all the time that is available to us before extinction. There is no other way except to start moving out of the solar system and start colonizing the galaxy.

EH (Edward Harrison): I am afraid we are not ready for that. I said this earlier, and I am reiterating again that the technological civilization on Earth has not yet reached a stage where it can understand and adequately implement a specific law called the 'Biogalactic Law', which is a requirement before we venture out to colonize the galaxy.

EW: And what is that biogalactic law?

EH: THE BIOGALACTIC LAW. We are the outcome of natural selection and the operation of this law can be attributed to the fitness of the human body and brain. Presumably, this is true also of the life on other planets that attains a state of advanced intelligence. When a civilization gains control of its planetary environment, the evolutionary game changes, however, and new rules determine what is fit and unfit.

Natural selection now operates on a planet-wide scale according to a biogalactic law that will be referred to as galactic selection. This speculative law of galactic selection states simply that "intelligent life-forms that are destructively aggressive do not colonize the galaxy". This law operates conceivably in two modes: the first is unconscious and automatic and the second is conscious and deliberate.

EW: The two words 'do not' in the pre-mentioned definition of the biogalactic law probably correspond to the five words, 'will not be permitted to'.

EH: Precisely. It goes without saying that the above objectives are indeed very difficult to achieve and even a very optimistic time frame far exceeds the time limit SW is setting for us. The technological civilization of Earth may have reached the top hundred in the Milky Way, but it may not reach the top ten if it self-destructs before that.

AE: Stephen, 200 years is rather pessimistic. But you are too optimistic that we can even start moving out from the planet, let alone colonize the galaxy within that time.

EH: The TC must survive many, many years (by avoiding self-destruction) to achieve this objective, develop interstellar space travel, develop fusion power and other technologies to construct large space vehicles that can travel at one-thousandth the speed of light, as well as have its own biosphere and contain a social unit of tens of thousands of people to enable 10000 years of travel time at a stretch by halting at one destination for 10000 years before embarking on the next journey. In this way, it is possible to diffuse outward at ten light-years per 20000 years and colonize a substantial portion of the galaxy. That's a long, long time indeed.

EW: And what happens to the humans if they become extinct?

SK: All eight or ten billion souls come out in the open or get stranded in interstellar space with nowhere to go to obtain consciousness again. Or maybe, they'll go into termites.

[Peter H. Diamandis, author of the bestselling book 'Abundance', takes the mic.]

PHD: You are terribly wrong in your assessment, Stephen Hawking. There is no need to panic at all. I have all the statistics available with me to show that—despite all the conflicts, wars, natural calamities, etc.— intelligence is well ahead of unintelligence. With every passing year, life spans are increasing and the quality of life is improving all the time. We—Steve Kotler (award-winning science writer) and I—have prepared documents to convincingly show how progress in artificial intelligence, robotics, infinite computing, ubiquitous broadband computing, digital manufacturing, nanomaterials, synthetic biology, and many other exponentially growing technologies will enable us to make more significant gains in the next 200 years. We will soon have the ability to meet and exceed the basic needs of every man woman and child on the planet. Abundance for all is within our grasp.

[Enter Martin Rees, scientist and cosmologist and author of the book 'Final Century'.]

MR: I am not in agreement with you, Peter. I have read *Abundance* in full and noticed that you didn't discuss the subject of nuclear wars at all, except for some cursory mentions here and there, and your coverage of global warming does not exceed a few sentences here and there. The increase in human life spans and the improvement in the quality of life are no yardsticks to measure the extent of time the human race can survive from extinction. A single button pressed by a harassed POTUS—or anyone—can lead to a chain reaction of scores of buttons pressed worldwide and that's it for the HR. I am in total agreement with Stephen Hawking. I don't think we have 200 years left. Perhaps the 21st century would be our FINAL CENTURY.

PHD: You may be right, Martin Rees, but I do have faith in the human instinct of self-preservation. Besides, I have full confidence in the success of this seminar.

[Yuval Noah Harari, author of another bestselling book 'Sapiens: A Brief History of Humankind', takes the mic.]

YNH: To satisfy both optimists and pessimists, we may conclude by saying that we are on the threshold of both heaven and hell, moving nervously between the gateway of one and the anteroom of the other. History has still not decided where we will end up and a string of coincidences might yet send us rolling in either direction.

[Many more hands are raised in the audience. But Einstein cuts short the interaction and takes the mike.]

AE: It seems there are conflicting views on what the future holds good for us. Can anyone provide a realistic assessment—assuming good sense remains generally elusive—of the time available before extinction so that we can make accurate and realistic plans to save ourselves without resorting to any knee jerk reactions?

SK: I will try to answer that question as best as I can commensurate with the quality and configuration of the brain cells supplied to me by the God who plays dice. I take the location of the needle—'X' minutes to midnight—of the Doomsday Emblematic Clock as determined by the Bulletin of Atomic Scientists as an authentic guideline to determine how dangerous the situation is. In 2015, while I was in the process of writing the manuscript of my book, *Intelligent Field*, I carried out a survey by inviting some friends to answer three questions. These friends of mine were reasonably knowledgeable and, by no means, experts on the subject. The three questions were:

Q1): What is the probable chance of a nuclear attack taking place anywhere in the world in one calendar year?

Q2): For each nuclear attack, what is the probable chance of a global chain reaction, leading to the extinction of the human race?

Q3): What is the probable chance that good sense will prevail and there will be no nuclear war in the next 500 years?

The weighted average—giving higher weight to the answers closest to the median—of the answers to the three questions were:

Answer to Q1: 1 in 300

Answer to Q2: 1 in 12

Answer to Q3: 1 in 10

In general, the participants were more optimistic that good sense would prevail and had faith in the human instinct of self-preservation. Their optimism corresponded more likely to a value of 'X' as five minutes before midnight even though the official value as per the Bulletin of Atomic Scientists at the time of the survey corresponded to 'X' as three minutes before midnight.

Thus 'Y' = 300 corresponded to a value of 'X' as five minutes before midnight.

Hence, the conclusion: 'Y' in figures is equal to 'X' in seconds.

Or 'Y' = 60'X', if 'X' is in minutes.

So if 'X' = two minutes as on date, as per the current status of the Bulletin of Atomic Scientist, 'Y' is worked out as 120.

This means the probable chance of a nuclear attack taking place somewhere on Earth in one year is 1 in 120, i.e., there is a 0.83% chance.

With regard to the answer to the second question, i.e., the probable chance of a chain reaction—following each nuclear attack—leading to the extinction of the human race, the average answer corresponded to a 1 in 12 probability. This needs to be corroborated by the great scientists and philosophers present here before I can proceed with the analysis to determine—in quantifiable terms—what lies ahead for us humans on Earth.

Some of the participants who took part in the survey are present here in the audience. I would like to request them to come forward with their views before I ask the scientists for their inputs.

AR (Lt. Gen. Arjun Ray): The dice seem to be loaded in favor of the doomsday scenario; however, for every pro-destruction theory, there is a counterhypothesis. My simple view is that, in a flat world, nuclear conflict is unlikely because the first-strike user will have to take the brunt of a counterstrike. This is why the Cold War era ended in favor of peace. Secondly, as the world gets more and more integrated, nuclear or biological catastrophes are unthinkable. Thirdly, given the increasing power of surveillance and countermeasures, such tragedies can be averted.

DM (Dharmesh Misra): My answers are clouded both by a hope that a nuclear war will never happen and by a fear of it happening. I believe, as per current geo-politics, nations with nuclear capability would not commence wars. At present, it is my hope and my guess that others, such as terrorist outfits, do not have the required capacity, unless, of course, they are provided facilities by some rogue nation. Even if a nuclear attack takes place, it will not set off a chain reaction or escalate to that level as other nations will come together to prevent it somehow. How? I do not know, but as Peter has pointed out, I have faith in the human instinct of self-preservation as all have seen the effects and have hopefully learned the lesson of Japan. The proof of it is in the Cuban Crisis, the Kargil War and so on. A full-scale global nuclear war is unlikely, in my opinion.

NB (Nitish Bhat): With China building up its arms capacity and high tensions between Russia and the United States (especially with respect to the crisis in the Middle East), I feel that a nuclear war is highly probable. Of course, I am a little pessimistic in my view here, in general, about mankind. Another possibility is that the nuclear weapons get into the hands of terrorists. With countries like Pakistan, which is growing weaker by the day in terms of civilian control, it is highly likely that extremists and terrorists will have access to its weapons sooner.

On the probability of a nuclear war converting into a chain reaction, I feel that it is highly probable that, once a war breaks out, it will quickly escalate into a mega-war, especially due to the existing alliances between powerful nations that are quite openly visible in their quests for self-protection and vested interests. We can argue here that nations will come together to stop a war rather than to elevate it into what would probably become World War III, especially due to the limitations that the nuclear weapons have put on tactical and diplomatic termination of wars and to the prevailing of man's natural instincts for peace and survival. But with the current breed of leaders at the helm of nations (especially the ones getting into position now), I highly doubt this possibility.

For my final answer, I am quite confused, actually. I want to be hopeful and optimistic about mankind's capacity to choose good over evil. I want to believe that there is a greater force in the nature that will prevent something like this (the wiping out of mankind) from occurring. At the same time, I feel that the world is never going to be free of nuclear weapons. Although the world as a whole is becoming closer and more compact by the day, the boundaries are becoming much more defined; ideologies are becoming much sterner and power much more concentrated. I would want to revisit these questions and my answers about ten years down the line to reflect on my understanding of man and the world and my current judgment.

NS (Nikhil Sagar): Mine is an optimistic view based on trusting that existing governance on nuclear (weapons) will continue and only get stronger.

CM (Dr. Clifton Meador): I certainly think the end could be leading toward self-destruction. I am not optimistic that we will be able to stop the destruction.

SN (Retd. Major Srinivas Nargolkar): I believe that the next nuclear exchange will be limited, causing tremendous destruction but not extinction.

MS (Mridula Sharma): I expect nuclear wars with chain reactions and devastation on a vast scale but no extinction. The world population will reduce to about 10%; thereafter, it will be a Golden Age for human beings.

SK: May I now ask the scientist to tell me what 'value' of this parameter I should take in my calculations?

AE: There are enormous complexities here and, as Stephen Hawking said, randomness is substantially widespread with wide variations in the possibilities; there is not enough information available to be able to predict what other nations would do in case of a nuclear attack. None of the scientists here can confidently say or predict what 'value' of this parameter should be used for the analysis. My suggestion is that we consider a range, such as, let's say, in the worst case scenario, we can take 'X' as two minutes to midnight as an answer to Q1 and 1 in 10 as the probable chance of a chain reaction leading toward extinction as the answer to Q2. And for the optimistic case, you start with 'X' as three minutes to midnight in the first millennium from now, progressively increasing—as intelligence and good sense keeps improving—to 12 minutes to midnight in the 10th millennium. And in all cases, you can take the value of the second parameter as 1 in 20. And let us say it will be safe thereafter.

SK: Thank you, sir. Here we go:

WORST CASE SCENARIO

Chances of surviving the next 100 years = $(1-1/120*10)^{100}$ = 92 %

Chances of surviving the next 500 years = $(1-1/120*10)^{500}$ = 66 %

Chances of Surviving the next 1000 years = $(1-1/120*10)^{1000}$ = 43.5 %

Chances of surviving the next 2000 years = $(1-1/1200)^{2000}$ = 19%

Chances of surviving the next 10000 years = $(1-1/1200)^{10000}$ = 2.4 %

So there is an 8% chance of human civilization becoming extinct in the next 100 years, a 56.5% chance of extinction in the next 1000 years and a nearly 98% chance of extinction in the next 10000 years.

OPTIMISITIC CASE SCENARIO

Chances of surviving the next 1000 years = $(1-1/180*20)^{1000}$ = 75.7 %

Chances of surviving the next 3000 years = $(1-1/240*20)^{3000}$ = 53.5 %

Chances of surviving the next 5000 years = $(1-1/300*20)^{5000}$ = 43.5 %

Chances of surviving the next 7000 years = $(1-1/360*20)^{7000}$ = 37.8 %

Chances of surviving the next 10000 years = $(1-1/450*20)^{10000} = 32.9\ \%$

So even in the optimistic case, there is a 24.3% chance of extinction in the next 1000 years, a 56.5% extinction chance in the next 5000 years and almost a 67.5% chance of extinction within the next 10000 years.

JW: Chilling thought. It goes without saying that something needs to be done on a war footing.

SK: Some people might call it a crude way of working, but I'll be glad to know if there is a better way. The trouble is no one is really doing any sort of calculation on this critical issue. Frankly, not many people in the world are really bothered about what lies ahead for the human race, which is the real tragedy.

[Janice Sinclaire, Communication Director of the Bulletin of Atomic Scientists, speaks up.]

JS: Thanks for the analysis, SK, but I must clarify that the clock is not a predictor of a nuclear attack. It is a metaphor for the end of humanity and the time is set by taking into account a variety of factors, including human-caused climate change and disruptive technologies.

SK: That makes it even more pessimistic. I corresponded with Janice over email on the subject. She also provided several links on the background of the clock and how it works. The articles referred to in the links were immensely useful in creating a better understanding of the subject and of the significant role played by the Bulletin Group toward peace in the world.

JS: For the past 70 years, the doomsday clock has served as a clarion call to all of us—scientists, policymakers, artists and ordinary citizens—to get engaged and help build a safer and healthier planet. The time for world leaders to address looming nuclear danger and the continuing march of climate change is long past. The time for citizens of the world to demand such action is now.

LDV: Can you update us on climate change, Janice?

[Enter Raymond Pierrehumbert (Halley Professor of Physics at the University of Oxford).]

RB: I will do that.

LDV: Please, go ahead.

RB: To halt global warming, the emission of carbon dioxide into the atmosphere by human activities such as fossil fuel burning, cement production and deforestation needs to be brought all the way to zero. The longer it takes to do so, the hotter the world will get. Lack of progress toward decarbonization has created justifiable panic about the climate crisis. This has led to an intensified interest in technological climate interventions that involve increasing the reflection of sunlight to space by injecting substances into the stratosphere, which leads to the formation of highly reflective particles. When first suggested, such albedo modification schemes were introduced as a "plan B" in case the world economy failed to decarbonize.

But because of the mismatch between the millennial persistence time of carbon dioxide and the sub-decadal persistence of stratospheric particles, albedo modification can never safely play more than a very minor role in the portfolio of solutions. There is simply no substitute for decarbonization.

Let's get this on the table right away without mincing words. With regard to the climate crisis, yes, it's time to panic.

We are in deep trouble.

To understand why, it is necessary to understand something about carbon budgets.

Some of the carbon dioxide added to the atmosphere by human activities, such as fossil fuel burning, is quickly taken up by the upper ocean and land ecosystems. Some of the rest is slowly absorbed into the deep ocean over the next millennium. However, a lot remains in the atmosphere, and it is only slowly removed by geological processes that take hundreds of thousands of years. Consequently, carbon dioxide accumulates in the atmosphere throughout the lifetime of the fossil-fueled economy, and it will not drop much even after we finally kick the carbon habit and cease our carbon dioxide emissions.

The situation is analogous to mercury accumulating throughout the lifetime of long-lived fish and the humans who eat them: It is cumulative exposure rather than the rate of exposure in any given year that determines the harm. Consequently, the longer the exposure persists, the closer one approaches a deadly accumulation.

So too with climate. Unlike conventional forms of pollution like those causing smog, which depend on local emission rates over the past week or so, the harm done to the climate by carbon dioxide emissions is determined by the cumulative emissions over spans of time measured in millennia. Since cumulative emissions by definition only go up, not down, the harm done by carbon dioxide emissions is, in effect, irreversible on time scales of importance to human societies. A corollary is that in order to halt global warming, *it is necessary to bring net carbon dioxide emissions by the world economy to zero.* There is no so-called 'safe' level of carbon dioxide emissions. As long as we continue emitting *any* carbon dioxide, the world will continue to warm.

Barring technological breakthroughs allowing for the active removal of massive amounts of carbon dioxide from the atmosphere, the cumulative carbon we emit will determine the climate our descendants will have to cope with for at least the next 10,000 years and probably much longer.

Cumulative carbon is usually expressed in terms of the amount of carbon contained in the carbon dioxide added to the atmosphere by fossil fuel burning, deforestation and similar human activities. That's because it is the carbon that is transferred to the atmosphere from long-standing reservoirs (primarily deeply buried fossil fuels) that we are concerned about; the oxygen in carbon dioxide was already in the atmosphere. A metric ton ("ton") of carbon dioxide, or about 2,200 pounds, contains a bit over a quarter-ton of carbon or about 550 pounds.

Anthracite coal is about 95 percent carbon, and gasoline and diesel fuel are about 86% carbon by weight, so completely burning a ton of either fossil fuel adds roughly 950 kilograms (kg) and 860 kg to the stock of cumulative carbon for which humanity is responsible.

What does this all mean?

The upshot is that the total cumulative carbon allocation for humanity compatible with a 50-50 chance of keeping global warming under 2 degrees Celsius (3.6 degrees Fahrenheit) is, in round numbers, a trillion tonnes.

That's it.

Forever.

And of that trillion tonnes, we have already used up over 630 billion tonnes, leaving just 370 billion tonnes to go.

That might seem like a lot of tonnes, but at current emissions rate, we'd get there in just 37 years, or 2057. Up until 2016, there was reason to hope that perhaps the world emission rate had stopped growing and had leveled off; if the emission rate held steady at that level out to 2030, and thereafter trended linearly to zero by 2080, then with the help of the Paris climate accords we would have decarbonized without exceeding the trillion-ton budget.

Sadly, those hopes have proved forlorn. While it is hazardous to draw conclusions about trends from just a few years of data, our recent carbon dioxide emissions record is gloomy; we are still on track for a perilous exponential growth rate. World emissions rose 1.5 percent in 2017, and an estimated 2.7 percent in 2018. For a time, US emissions continued to decline modestly despite the Trump Administration's environmental vandalism; the inexorable forces of the market meant that aging coal-fired power plants continued to be replaced by cheaper, cleaner, newer, and more efficient plants powered by natural gas and renewables. But growing carbon dioxide emissions due to industry and transportation have more than offset this progress, leading to an estimated 3.4 percent growth in US emissions in 2018. Chinese emissions went up nearly 2 percent in 2017 and 4.7 percent in 2018—even while China put into place aggressive domestic energy policies in the past few years, which may, eventually, bring down their national emissions. In addition, their "Belt and Road" foreign infrastructure initiative—involving the creation of a vast, $1.3 trillion network of railways, energy pipelines, power plants, highways and border crossings that seeks to create a China-led trading bloc involving two-thirds of the world's population—is also funding a great deal of harmful fossil fuel development, including $20 billion in funding for coal plants around the world.

Even in the European Union, which has expressed a strong commitment to decarbonization, emissions were up 1.8 percent in 2017, resulting in little progress toward decarbonization. Every year that passes where emissions fail to decrease puts the goal of staying under a trillion tonnes farther out of reach.

With continued 2.5 percent compound growth, we hit our trillion-ton limit in under 27 years. And if the trend continues beyond that time, the dark magic of exponential growth brings our planet to two trillion tonnes in 50 years (4 degrees Celsius of warming, or 7.2 degrees Fahrenheit) and three trillion tonnes (6 degrees Celsius warming, or roughly 10.8 degrees Fahrenheit) just 86 years from now. Just 2 degrees Celsius of warming would have been bad enough; 4 degrees Celsius of global warming would be "cataclysmic," said a report by the World Bank. The impacts are familiar: increased forest fires, drought in some places but deluges in others, loss of Arctic sea ice, increase in deadly heatwaves, increased food insecurity, sea-level rise and biodiversity loss, among many other impacts—and we know for certain that the hotter it gets, the worse it gets.

And land warms more than the global average, and Arctic warming is even more amplified than land warming. An additional consideration is that there's a 50–50 chance that the warming is worse than these mid-range forecasts, perhaps *much* worse. Heat stress could make half the planet uninhabitable for mammals outdoors.

That's all unquestionably bad news. The question is not whether to panic, but how to respond constructively to the entirely justifiable anxiety about the climate disruption we are bringing upon ourselves.

Solutions? Or false premises?

And that brings us around to the basket of attempted climate fixes loosely, if inappropriately, referred to as "geoengineering," and specifically to schemes to cool the Earth by increasing its reflection of sunlight back to space (otherwise known as its albedo).

This sort of climate intervention is usually referred to by its boosters as "solar radiation management" or "solar geoengineering," but regardless of which term is used, they both give the false impression of a comforting level of precision in knowing the outcome—something that is wholly inappropriate in the face of the substantial uncertainties surrounding it. We simply do not know the way the climate will respond to these novel forcings, or how our social and political systems will respond to these disruptive and possibly ungovernable technologies. At present, it looks like the most feasible means of albedo hacking, from a purely technical standpoint, is the injection of substances into the stratosphere that lead to the formation of tiny aerosol particles that effectively reflect sunlight.

Albedo hacking has been touted as a sort of plan B to make up for the world's failure to make a responsible start on decarbonization of the economy. But of all the possible scenarios in which albedo hacking would be deployed, using it to make up for a failure to decarbonize is the most nonsensical. Carbon dioxide accumulates in the atmosphere, but stratospheric aerosols do not. Therefore, albedo hacking as a response to a failure to decarbonize requires injecting ever-increasing amounts of chemicals into the stratosphere, up to the point where the physical limits of the technique are reached or unanticipated adverse consequences become unbearable.

The excess carbon dioxide that human activities inject into the atmosphere has a warming effect that extends essentially forever, whereas the stratospheric aerosols meant to offset that warming fall out of the atmosphere in about a year. It's just a matter of gravity—stuff denser than its surroundings falls—aided a bit by atmospheric circulations that enhance the removal. This is why the cooling effects of even a major volcanic eruption like Pinatubo dissipate after two years or so. Hence, whatever level of albedo hacking is needed to avoid a dangerous level of warming must be continued essentially forever.

Otherwise, an abrupt termination would catastrophically unleash pent-up warming in a matter of a few years—a snapback known as termination shock—and the magnitude of this potential climate shock would increase, the longer that albedo hacking is used to offset our failure to decarbonize. Deployment of albedo hacking does not in any way "buy time" to get carbon dioxide emissions under control since, once emitted, carbon dioxide cannot to any significant extent be un-emitted with known economically feasible technology; if albedo modification becomes necessary, it must be maintained essentially forever. The problematic need to continue albedo hacking essentially forever, if it becomes necessary at all, is called the problem of millennial commitment.

Forever.

Think of what that word means: We would be committing generations yet unborn to continuously run a mechanical process, over a time-span longer than the age of the pyramids.

And if our offspring don't (or simply can't) do so at some point in the future, then they will suffer the consequences of an unimaginably huge climate shock, accumulated over vast amounts of time.

And to be clear, let it be noted here that I am not against benign, failure-tolerant, supplementary approaches to dealing with climate change, such as planting massive numbers of trees to help remove more carbon from the atmosphere—I just think that such so-called "natural" solutions have been oversold by the mass media. Their contributions, while useful, will be minor.

Where do we go from here?

The first order of business is to double down on efforts to decarbonize.

There is still time to turn that around—and if we don't, any attempt to patch the climate using albedo hacking will only make the problem worse through the ever-increasing risk of termination shock.

To decarbonize, however, requires building a political movement that regards the climate crisis as a top priority. The Extinction Rebellion movement in the United Kingdom and the "Skolstrejk" actions led by young Greta Thunberg have helped to create a justified sense of urgency, and there are signs of an awakening in the US Democratic Party in the form of the push for a Green New Deal.

The United Kingdom, despite a conservative government and a dysfunctional Parliament tied in knots over Brexit, has managed to make a legally enforceable commitment to achieve net zero carbon emissions by 2050 and has made significant progress toward that goal.

Then, too, there is a potential role for the more benign forms of climate intervention, namely Carbon Dioxide Removal (CDR), which would actively remove carbon dioxide from the air and store it in some form or place from which it could not get back. CDR is benign, in the sense that it does not treat just the symptom of the climate crisis but its root cause, and it does not have the problem of termination shock or millennial commitment.

CDR may never be economically feasible, so it would be dangerous to count on it as a fix, but it would be a valuable element of the portfolio of responses if it ever became feasible; it deserves vastly expanded research funding relative to the trickle of funding it gets currently.

It should be cautioned, though, that the emerging fad for so-called natural approaches to CDR is largely wishful thinking, and can play only a minor role relative to decarbonization.

There is also a lot of hype surrounding the potential for improved agricultural practices to take carbon dioxide out of the atmosphere and store the carbon in soils. But carbon stored in soil is not separated from the oxygen that wants to recombine with it, and there is a limit to the extent of storage. In pasturelands, researchers have estimated that soils could take up at most 200 million tonnes of carbon per year, but the reservoir would saturate after a few decades. Even allowing for 50 years of storage, which amounts to a measly 10 billion tonnes of carbon—just about one year of current emissions.

There is simply no good fix if we fail to stop pumping carbon into the atmosphere. We are already suffering some of the harms due to human-caused climate disruption. The only question is how much we will ratchet up the toll of human suffering, and the destruction of the ecosystems with which we share the Earth before we finally achieve net zero carbon emissions.

EW: Which means, essentially, there is no plan B.

RB: Yes, no plan B. That is precisely what I have been trying to say.

PHD: My optimism, in *Abundance*, was based on the assumption that plan A would take care of the crisis and that no plan B would be required. That the trillion-ton budget won't be exceeded and that we will reach net zero emission by 2100.

EW: That 'intelligence' will conquer the 'unintelligence' at least on the climate front.

MR: It's a tall order, at least in my view.

AE: Thank you, Raymond. That was nice and elaborate.

EW: After all is said and done, where will the needle be placed when the atomic scientists meet next in January 2020?

SK: If no improvement is seen, it will not be further away from one and a half minutes to midnight.

AE: And the worst case scenario?

SK: In recent weeks, we hear provocative statements from the Pakistan PM and the words 'nuclear war' are being heard repeatedly.

AE: In which case?

SK: It could well be one minute to midnight.

LDV: Thank you, all. I will now ask Einstein to present his concluding thoughts on the seminar and the proposed solutions to the problems faced by the human race. After that, in the final session, I will ask some of the world leaders who were invited to this second day of the seminar and who very kindly consented to be present to please come on the stage and provide their views as well as their intent.

[Before Einstein takes the mic, many hands are raised as the audience tries to get a chance to speak.]

LDV: There is time for just one more. It should relate to finding practical solutions. *[Selects one person at random and invites him to come on the stage.]*

AKC (A. K. Chandrashekhar) *[takes the mike]*: The dynamics of people's and leaders' attitudes toward peace and the survival of the world are important. Though democracies have a greater tendency to ensure peace in the long run, in the short-term, democracies can throw into seats of power men, like Hitler, Mussolini, Reagan, Bush and now Trump, who are all products of popular elections. How does one limit their potential for harm to the world and its survival? One great suggested solution is to contain nationalism through the strengthening of international institutions like the United Nations with increased empowerment of all nations in global decision-making without special privileges to a handful of nations, like the Security Council members with their veto powers. Nuclear powers try ineffectively to prevent other countries from becoming nuclear powers; the hypocrisy of it all is inherent in their attempts.

Through a well-empowered United Nations, as proposed, all nations can try and persuade and/or oblige the nuclear powers to place their entire nuclear arsenals at the disposal of the UN, which can effectively defuse the arsenal in a mutually agreed-upon manner. The risk of nuclear war can be reduced to a level near-zero in a single generation. Parallel with this course, the risk of all wars is high in different parts of the world because of free international trade of arms, largely from the large armament-manufacturing nations, like the United States, the United Kingdom, Germany, France, Sweden, South Africa, Israel, Russia, China, India, and so forth, to the rest of the world through deals mired with corruption, stinking to the skies. International trade of arms can be totally banned so that this blood trade and attendant corruption are stopped with a steep reduction in the risk of wars to near-zero levels.

The United Nations can then enforce the disbanding of standing armies in all nations with a fraction of the total strength of the national armed forces being kept under the United Nations on a proportional conscription basis for maintaining world peace. The United Nations can next ensure that, within nations, autocracies and dictatorships do not act despotically against their own peoples by sending its peacekeeping forces to quell civil strife and supervise their transitions to peaceful democracies. The above reforms in international governance cannot begin at the initiative of the present day leading powers like the United States, the United Kingdom, Germany, France, Russia and China, who are themselves power-mongering nations. They have to be brought about by rational and/or peace-loving individuals in every walk of life, be they in business, service, science, arts, government, bureaucracy, judiciary, education, religion, or even in the armed forces, for that matter.

All individuals interested in world peace can organize themselves into national groups to persuade their own leaders and people in positions of national importance. These national groups could send their most effective representatives to a strong international group that can maintain dialogues with national governments, the United Nations and opinion builders across nations interested in international peace and progress, where all differences of opinion are settled through dialogue, debate, appeal to reason, humanity and fair play between peoples and nations. The original founders of the Pugwash movement, like Bertrand Russell, did have proposals similar to the above for ensuring world peace free from the threat of all wars in general and nuclear wars in particular.

I would not try to reduce the risks of war through an opinion poll about the perception of people regarding the risk of war and peace. If a microscopic fraction of space in the universe has life like that on Earth with intelligence and conscience, it can also develop its own capability for surviving its limitations by purposefully working for it rather than leaving its survival to the outcome of an opinion poll, when what is needed is change of opinions for world's peace, survival and prosperity. I see the germ of such a solution developing from the present crisis of refugees from the Middle East entering Europe for succor from war.

Through goodwill, people of different faiths and their national governments are offering to help the refugees in their hour of a man-made crisis. All of them can work together so that the roots of such a crisis are removed forever from our midst. Instead of a clash of civilizations, we can have virtuous cooperation of civilizations to bridge our differences and deliver the world from its wars and conflicts for common good, survival, peace and progress.

LDV: Thank you, Chandrashekhar. Over to Einstein for the concluding thoughts on the seminar.

AE: Thank you, Leonardo, for inviting me to present my concluding thoughts. Thank you, Erwin Schrodinger, John Wheeler, Eugene Wigner and many other greats assembled here for their invaluable contributions to the seminar. My heartfelt appreciation and congratulations are due to the National Institute of Advanced Studies, Bangalore for having assumed the responsibility to bring this superb symposium into being, manage its evolution so well and facilitate its transmission to a wider world so effectively.

May I begin with an article of political faith? It runs as follows: The State is made for man, not man for the State. I regard it as the chief duty of the state to protect the individual and give him the opportunity to develop into a creative personality. That is to say, the State should be our servant and not we its slaves. The State transgresses this commandment when it compels us by force to engage in military and war service, the more so since the object and the effect of this slavish service is to kill people belonging to other countries or interfere with their freedom of development. We are only to make such sacrifices to the State as will promote the free development of individual human beings. It is hoped that the fight against war will find strong support among the peoples of the State including those of the State of America.

In this connection, I am in total agreement with Chandrashekhar that nationalism must be contained by strengthening international institutions. In my view, the greatest obstacle to international order is that monstrously exaggerated spirit of nationalism, which also goes by the fair-sounding but misused name of patriotism. During the last two centuries, this idol has acquired an uncanny and exceedingly pernicious power everywhere. The present deplorably high development of nationalism everywhere is, in my opinion, intimately connected with the institution of compulsory military service or, to call it by its sweeter name, national armies.

A state which demands military service of its inhabitants is compelled to cultivate in them a nationalistic spirit, thereby laying the psychological foundation for their military usefulness. The introduction of compulsory military service is, therefore, to my mind, the prime cause of the moral decay of the white race, which seriously threatens not merely the survival of our civilization, but our very existence. Again, I agree with Chandrashekhar when he says, "Instead of a clash of civilizations, we can have virtuous cooperation of civilizations to bridge our differences and deliver the world from its wars and conflicts for common good, survival, peace and progress."

But this is not happening.

Because some states have turned into deep states; this is true for America and, to some extent, Pakistan and a few other countries. Every informed person is aware of the deep state's role in 9/11. All the living presidents of the US know it. Most world leaders know it. Vladimir Putin knows it and is in possession of satellite pictures in support. Structural engineers, architects, and expert pilots and lawyers of the world know it.

But it is still considered as an 'unpatriotic conspiracy theory' even though we cannot discredit the evidence—as Sherlock Holmes has pointed out—that lies in the statement: 'Newton's third law of motion cannot be violated'. Clearly, the evidence is compelling, and it can put the US Attorney in an unenviable position.

How do we resolve the problem?

That is the question. Now, there are many deep states on the planet and many problems other than those attributed to it. In my view, which is very much in consonance with the view of the great scientists assembled here, these problems should not be solved in isolation. The solution of these great problems will come together. Just as, in understanding nature—as pointed out by Lee Smolin—a possible way forward is to give up the attempt to apply quantum theory to the universe as a whole and to regard quantum theory as the record of quantum information that one subsystem may have about another subsystem as a result of their mutual interaction. In the same way, concerning the deep states, the interconnectedness between the problems must be thoroughly investigated, understood and resolved holistically, such that the solution of one problem should not lead to the creation of another. For example, if the deep state is somehow brought under control and is unable to stage-manage any more wars and conflicts in the Middle East or elsewhere, what will the million-strong American army do and how will the Major Corporations and the Defense Contractors of the MIC survive?

Nevertheless, the future security of the human race should not be left to the revolving doors of chance. It must be planned meticulously with no scope for miscalculations. Just as the universe is a designed universe with immaculately designed constants of nature incorporated beautifully into the laws of science to enable life and consciousness to appear and then understand the universe. In the same way, the actions of human beings (particularly of leaders of nations) should be meticulously designed to enable solutions to all the problems in a subtle manner and in a congenial atmosphere and from a neutral perspective and not the perspective of this or that nation or religion or culture.

As we all know, the current geopolitical situation in the world is such that the assumption of an approximate 1 in 120 chance of a nuclear war taking place in a calendar year— as estimated by SK based on the emblematic clock at two minutes to midnight— may not be an incorrect assumption. If it is indeed somewhat incorrect, it may need an upward revision rather than a downward revision. The situation is serious enough to force the realization that there are no options other than a collective approach by the leaders of the world's nations to come together and address all the problems with an integrated approach.

It is profoundly imminent that at some time in the future, this realization will manifest itself. It remains to be seen if that happens before the first nuclear war or after the first, second or third such war. Nations in conflict should become aware of these possibilities and understand the consequences of not resolving their disputes quickly. Leaders of these conflicting nations must come together with a positive attitude and a neutral perspective and address their problems in the same way as a neutral person, such as an alien being from outer space, would have done.

How would such a neutral figure (let's call him 'F'), who has watched all the proceedings and has complete knowledge and understanding of all the conflicts on Earth address the problems in a way that is as far as possible acceptable to all concerned? It is assumed, of course, that 'F' understands human nature and is perfectly aware that a typical human being, anywhere in the world, wants to live in peace and that the average moral standard is the same in all countries and does not differ from country to country as it is not a measure of 'temperature' or 'humidity'.

The average quotient 'qx' pertaining to the desire to 'live and let live' is also generally the same for all countries, provided the corresponding quotient 'qy' pertaining to the leaders of the country is greater than or at least equal to 'qx'. Our man understands science and the laws of causation. He fully understands that it is the interactions of the world that lead to the coming together of millions of atoms and molecules and arrives as a speck of jelly; it is the same phenomena responsible for the said speck of jelly to go on to become either Hitler, Gandhi, Leonardo or you and me.

Each of us is subject to a specific and unique set of interactions or memories of which keep getting stored in our brains; all our actions are dictated by these interactions.

Carrying forward this logic our man, therefore, understands that a person with a substantially small 'qx' value (a murderer or a terrorist, for example) is not responsible for his actions. But from practical considerations, it is advisable not to have tea with him. The only way out is by raising his 'intelligence' to a level that exceeds his 'ego' by remote control means through a proper understanding of his past interactions that caused his 'qx' to fall.

In view of the above, while the word 'terrorism' may still be used, the word 'terrorist' should henceforth be replaced by a set of three words viz 'Misunderstood Human Being (MHB)' as these terrorists happen to be victims of time.

With all this, it does not serve the purpose if we call a certain country, which is just a geographical area, a terrorist state and another country, another geographical area, a 'selfish and arrogant policeman' when we know that it is the leaders of nations who must be held responsible for bringing their nations to such disrepute.

Therefore 'F' should first understand how the common man from the various countries finds himself entangled in these complex and dangerous situations for no fault of his and how he can be extricated from these entangled states.

'Intelligence' must conquer the 'unintelligence'.

Now there are two categories of 'unintelligence' that need to be taken care of. Category one corresponds to and is attributed to a lack of knowledge and understanding of the subject, but where the intent is not bad, such as that relating to climate change, on whether there is a plan B, such as Albedo Hacking or CDR, etc., other than doubling down on decarbonization. This category of 'unintelligence' should be easily taken care of by science and the expertise of the scientist. But it is the second category of 'unintelligence', which is attributed to poor intent, selfishness, arrogance and egoism, particularly of leaders of nations, is dangerous and must be taken care of without any further delay.

However, even the second category of 'unintelligence' needs be conquered by 'intelligence' without the necessity of calling a particular nation or a specific individual unintelligent. A nation is just a geographical area and an individual is just a mind and it's the same mind in all individuals, as very nicely explained by Schrodinger in his talk on the 'Oneness of the Mind'.

Self-realization—by the leaders of nations—of one's past mistakes and a willingness and readiness to make amends must be the approach to be followed. Thus, if I were the president of the US and patiently watched the video of this seminar and heard and assimilated the views of the great scientists and philosophers assembled here, I would have no hesitation in accepting my past mistakes—such as withdrawing from the Iran Nuclear Deal and the Paris Accord on Climate Change, to name just a few—and try to make amends as much as possible. 99% of the world will approve this and I believe the remaining 1% will also approve it if they have watched this seminar.

[Note: Einstein is not aware that Donald Trump was one of the world leaders Leonardo invited. The invited personalities

are wearing masks and will only remove them when asked to come on stage.]

Next, if I was the leader of the Sunni Saudi Arabia and you *[looks at Schrodinger]* were the leader of the Shia Iran, we would have no hesitation whatsoever in shaking our hands and resolving our differences. Frankly speaking, as a scientist who understands relativity, I could not understand what these differences are. A united Islam is way better than a divided Islam. And a united Islam has a much better chance of peaceful coexistence with other religions, keeping in mind the essence of religion, as outlined earlier, as well as the oneness of the mind.

Next, I could be the leader of Pakistan and you *[looks at John Wheeler]* were the leader of India and so on. Not forgetting I need to accept my past mistakes and the necessity to make amends for it, even though there were valid reasons for doing what I did. My part in producing the atomic bomb consisted of a single act. I signed a letter to President Roosevelt, pressing the need for experiments on a large-scale in order to explore the possibilities for the production of an atomic bomb.

I was fully aware of the terrible danger to mankind in case this attempt succeeded. But the likelihood that the Germans were working on the same problem with a chance of succeeding forced me to this step. I could do nothing else, although I have always been a convinced pacifist. To my mind, to kill in war is not a whit better than to commit ordinary murder.

As long as, however, the nations are not resolved to abolish war through common actions and to solve their conflicts and protect their interests through peaceful decisions on a legal basis, they feel compelled to prepare for war. They feel obliged to prepare all possible *means* even the most detestable ones so as not to be left behind in the general armament race. This road necessary leads to war, a war that, under the present conditions, means universal destruction.

Under these circumstances, the fight against means has no chance of success. Only the radical abolition of wars and of the threat of war can help. This is what one has to work for. One has to be resolved not to let himself be forced to actions that run counter to this goal. This is a severe demand on an individual who is conscious of his dependence on society. But it is not an impossible demand.

Gandhi, the great genius, has pointed the way. He has shown what sacrifices people are capable of once they find the right way. His work for the liberation of India is a living testimony to the fact that a will governed by firm conviction is stronger than seemingly invincible material power.

On the question of what should be done about the deep states of the world, one has to realize that the powerful industrial groups concerned in the manufacture of arms are doing their best in all countries to prevent the peaceful settlement of international disputes and that rulers can only achieve this great end if they are sure of the vigorous support of the majority of their people. In these days of democratic government, the fate of nations hangs on the people themselves; each individual must always bear that in mind.

May the conscience and the common sense of the peoples be awakened so that we may reach a new stage in the life of nations, where people will look back on war as an incomprehensible aberration of their forefathers.

LDV: That was wonderful, Einstein. Thank you very much.

We have with us some surprise visitors as guest speakers. They are here in person or over a conference call. I will now invite them to come on the stage and give their presentations and enlighten us with their plans and intents. To begin with, I call upon a few Misunderstood Human Beings, victims of time.

[The lights go out, the curtains come down and the music keeps playing but the tone changes. Lights, of a different color, are switched on one by one. The curtain slowly rises again.

Six leaders of organizations, such as Al-Qaeda, ISIS, LeT, Taliban, etc., appear on the screen. Believe it or not, there is applause to welcome them. Then one of the six comes forward and takes center stage to give his presentation. He is a changed man. So are all the others who represent 'the tainted ones'.]

MUB: Even in our wildest dreams, we could not have imagined that we would get an opportunity like this to explain to the world why some of us did things we shouldn't have done. The history of at least the last 70 years or so, along with a serious understanding of the law of causation and the interactions theory, as explained by Mr. Einstein, must be taken into consideration in order to understand why some of us did things we should not have done. Then we will decide0 on the course of action that the world leaders must take to ensure the future security of human beings.

It is true that we, human beings, are the outcome of natural selection and the operation of this law can be attributed to the fitness of the human body and brain. But this law cannot be operated by improving the fitness of one section of human society at the cost of causing suffering to another section. The evolutionary game must change. Interference is not the answer; a global approach and cooperation is the answer.

Ours (a part of 'us') was indeed a wrong hand, and we were on our way to doing things that we might not do now as a consequence of having understood the interactions theory and the oneness of the mind, as was nicely explained by Mr. Schrodinger, but I would like to say: the 'responsibility toward the future security of the world lies not just in preventing wrong hands from getting powerful but also in preventing powerful hands from possible wrong actions'.

[Then one by one, some leaders of nations in conflict take the stage and explain themselves. Then they give suggestions. The consensus that emerges is that 'the Three Divides' must be brought to a minimum: The divide 'between the rich and the poor', the divide 'between the West and Islam' and, above all, the divide 'between the various factions of the Muslim world'.

The view that emerges is that the problems of the world that needed to be dealt with are deprived societies, rogue governments, dispersed militias, corruption in high places, rampant thuggery, etc. The view that emerges next is that the nuclear arsenal of the world must be destroyed as early as possible. What comes next is that the trouble makers must now become the trouble shooters.

A group of five Republican Senators comes on the screen next. One of them takes the mic.]

RS1:   Donald Trump is our president. He has played his part in accordance with the cards dealt to him. Scientists with an acute understanding of the law of causation will agree with me that there was no way he could have played them differently. After all is said and done, it depends on the interactions of the world on him, as beautifully explained by Einstein.

Yes, it is true, he was installed by Putin as POTUS, and there was no way he could not have been friendly with Putin. The purpose of helping Trump to the presidential seat was to take care of the deep state of America, which is considered by Russia and China as dangerous for the world. Both Russia and China are prepared to confront the USA in war, as very elaborately explained by CFT and DOA. The USA was well aware of this, as is clear from the November 2015 Nuclear Test (*Bright Light In The Sky*) carried out by the US, considered by experts as nothing other than a $31 million billboard warning to Russia and China, saying, "DON'T MEDDLE (…) WITH US."

So if a war against Russia has been prevented from happening for the last three years, we should have no hesitation in attributing this as a success for Trump at least to some extent. Other than this, I cannot find anything that Trump has done that deserves praise. He could not make any headway in controlling the deep state. By befriending Saudi Arabia and the other Sunni states in the Middle East and turning them against Iran, imposing and then increasing sanctions on Iran and, above all, withdrawing from the Iran Nuclear Deal, Trump has very much played into the hands of the deep state.

Recently, he befriended Erdogan, the President of Turkey (the original deep state). He then announced the withdrawal of US troops from Kurdish-held territory in Northern Syria and opened up space for Turkey to attack the Kurds. Trump considered this as a wise step and emphatically claimed it victory for him. Never mind if it was a dramatic setback for the US' strategic and humanitarian priorities in Syria, never mind if the US is now unable to secure the territorial defeat of ISIS and prevent its resurgence, never mind if the US is currently unable to provide a secure space with humanitarian relief for the diverse community of Christians, Kurds and others in the region who have looked to America for support, never mind if the US has now lost its credibility.

To cut a long story short, it was expected to be "Trump vs. the deep state". But it turned out to be "Trump + the deep state".

His withdrawal from the Paris Accord on climate change was an absolutely terrible decision. This decision, if not reversed soon, can have catastrophic consequences on the environment.

I could go on and on but there is no need. I think the 'information in the field', as elaborately put forward by CFT and DOA, should be enough. And now President Donald Trump is facing impeachment. It's a colossal waste of everybody's time, not to mention the taxpayers' money. I suggest he step down to save himself the blushes.

[Another Republican Senator took the mic from RS1.]

RS2:   They say it is unlikely to obtain a two-thirds majority in the Senate to be able to remove Donald Trump from office. But I say it is possible, especially if the senators have all seen the recording of this seminar. I suggest Trump should step down. But he should be given ample time to make amends. Under no circumstances should he contest the 2020 Election.

[One by one, the remaining three Republican Senators voice their views. They all suggest Trump step down and not contest the 2020 election. They say he should be given three months to make good the damage he has done and re-join the Paris Accord as well as the Iran Nuclear Deal.]

LDV: I now invite Donald Trump, the honorable President of the United States of America, to come on board, please.

[All eyes turn to the screen as Trump slowly arrives and takes the mic.]

DT: ET TU, REPUBLICANS. THEN FALL TRUMP!

I played my part strictly, as required by the laws of causation, and I am playing my part now by saying, "I RESIGN THE GAME."

Yes, I played my part to perfection. I prevented Russia and China from attacking us. Don't blame me if they attack now. I ushered in the Stock Market Boom. Don't blame me if it crashes now. I first threatened and then made friends with Kim Jong Un and prevented him from Bombing us. Don't blame me if he changes his mind now. Anyway, I will still make sure he denuclearizes even if I have to remove the sanctions. I think I'll do that. Or maybe I won't, we'll see. In the same way, I threatened Iran, and believe me, I was going to shake hands with their leader, what's his name? I may still do so, or will I? I don't know. We'll see about that.

Now, if there is an impeachment, I tell you there will be a civil war in America. But that won't happen as I am resigning from the game and saving America. That's it.

God help me and God help America. God help the world.

LDV: Thank you, Mr. Trump.

DT: Not so easy, Leonardo. I want you to send your painting, MONA LISA, to be hung in my drawing room.

EW: QUID PRO QUO.

EPILOGUE

Q&A in a parallel universe

Q: Recall the conversation between John Wheeler and Eugene Wigner and Wheeler's words: "Events so numerous and so uncoordinated that flaunting their freedom from the formula, they yet fabricate firm form. The universe is a self-excited circuit. As it expands, cools and develops, it gives rise to observer-participancy. Observer-participancy, via the mechanism of the delayed-choice experiment, in turn gives what we call tangible reality to the universe. Of all the strange features of the universe, none are stranger than these: time is transcended, laws are mutable and observer-participancy matters". What is the significance of these words?

A: Wheeler's philosophy of science is much more radically relativistic than Einstein's. Wheeler would make all physical laws relative to observers. He has us creating physical laws by our existence. In principle, if the role of observers in the universe is as essential as he imagines, life may even create physical laws by conscious decision.

Q: What is a self-excited circuit?

A: Starting small, the universe grows (loop of U) and in time, gives rise to observer-participancy, which in turn imparts 'tangible reality' to even the earliest days of the universe. In order to understand this, we must first understand the mechanism of an experiment called the ***'Delayed-choice experiment'***.

Q: Can you explain the delayed-choice experiment?

A: This is a thought experiment conceptualized by John Wheeler. To grasp this, let us go back to the double-slit experiment with electrons. Consider that a new detector screen is set up somewhere in between the two holes and the last detector screen. Now, in accordance with the quantum theory, if we decide to turn off this new detector, there will be an interference pattern formed in the main detector. On the other hand, if we decide to ***delay*** our choice of looking and look only after the electron has passed the two hole screen by activating/or installing the new detector—by means of a fast computer—only at that stage, we find that there is no interference pattern. Actual experiments have, in fact, been carried out in the Universities of Maryland in the US and Munich, Germany, to confirm this astounding phenomenon.

Q: How does this happen? What in the world is going on and what does this mean?

A: It appears that this delayed decision seems to have affected how the electron behaved when it was in the process of passing through the hole(s) a tiny fraction of a second (perhaps a billionth of a second) in the past.

Q: Isn't that a violation of our notion of causality?

A: It is in this sense that quantum mechanics does strange things to what we call causality if we examine it with sufficient care. Hence, it is in this sense that there is no such thing as a causality violation paradox. It is just that we need a better understanding of the laws of nature. At a certain level, there must be a transformation in the law. We do not understand the mechanism of the transformation, but we do know that a transformed law of science is NOT violated.

Q: But how far can we go back in the past? What is the relevance of the example of the delayed-choice experiment to the question, with regard to galaxies appearing at the horizon? How would it be possible for an observer to influence them?

A: In the words of John Wheeler, "I have mentioned the delayed-choice double-slit experiment but perhaps I have not spoken sufficiently vividly about it in the sense that the experiment in which we were talking about it was the one in which the interval between the metal plate with two holes in it and the place with the Venetian blinds where we make our choice—we'll say one foot or time of one nanosecond—but there is nothing in principle to prevent it being a billion light-years in the sense that we in the here and now, by observing a photon of the primordial cosmic fireball radiation, have an irretrievable consequence for what we have the right to say about the photon. In that sense, we are operating in the reverse direction of the sense of time and it is in that sense that anything having to do with things swimming up over the horizon also comes into this category of events."

So the timescales involved need not be so tiny, and we can imagine a similar experiment on a literally cosmic scale. Consider for example, light from a distant object, such as a quasar, arrives after having traversed two different routes after getting bent around a massive galaxy in the line of sight—the phenomenon is known as gravitational lensing—the two quasar images can be combined to make an interference pattern to prove that the light traveled across the universe like a wave following both routes. However, if we monitor individual photons to check which route they traversed, there is no such interference pattern. Now the quasar might be 10 billion light-years away, but we have timed our observation today and it has affected the way the light set out on its journey 10 billion years ago.

Q: This is very difficult to believe.

A: Yes, of course, it is difficult to believe. But so is 'Time Dilation', 'Length contraction', 'Lorentz transformation', not forgetting 'Quantum entanglement' and 'The Interconnectedness of the universe'.

Q: Not to mention the traveling Cosmic Mind?

A: Yes, and its ability to travel back in time so as to remain forever in the livable eras of the universe, such as the Stelliferous era where stars are shining and life and consciousness are flourishing.

Q: And not to proceed toward the Degenerate eras, the Black-Hole Eras, and the Dark Eras of the deep future, where it cannot obtain consciousness, hence, meaningless to go there?

A: Precisely.

Q: So if this Omnipresent cosmic mind—Omnipresent in space as well as time—decides to go back to the past, say to the year 1900, will the events of the 20th century be the same as they actually happened in this universe?

A: No way. The probability of that would be just about as low as the probability of an aircraft being assembled by a tornado striking a junkyard.

Q: So no WW1 and no WW2?

A: Maybe not. Or maybe there'd be four world wars. What do I know?

Q: On what would that depend?

A: On the visions and ideas transmitted to the human minds of the past, based on the experience gained and the inputs received via the information in the intelligent field of the intervening period between the year 1900 and the present, by the traveling cosmic mind before it decides to go back to the year 1900.

Q: So if it turns out that there are catastrophic wars in the future and huge problems brought about by climate change, and the Emblematic Doomsday clock finds itself at just a few seconds away from midnight and human civilization on the verge of extinction, say 200 years from now, and if the traveling Cosmic mind decides to travel back to the present moment, what would the visions and ideas required to be transmitted to the intelligent human minds of the present be?

A: Good question. I guess these ideas maybe something like this:

Dismantle the deep states of the world, particularly that of America.

Dismantle the conflicts of the world, especially the conflicts between the Shias and the Sunnis.

Dismantle religious extremism and the intolerance of other religions

Converge all religions into a single religion whose essence is peaceful coexistence, to live and let live and to take care of the environment around us.

Q: In short, SWITCH OFF the deep states of the world and SWITCH ON the good times for the lives on the planet.

A: Yes. Thank you.

Q: Wait, I'm not finished yet. I have a few more questions.

A: Go on.

Q: What is the meaning and significance of the equation E= m*c^2?

A: About 30 million quarks collided with the same number (except one) of antiquarks in each neighborhood during that first microsecond of the Big Bang. The collision resulted in the annihilation of all quarks and antiquarks, except that one quark that could not find its antiquark. You and I are made up of such surplus quarks that could not be annihilated and so we arrived in the universe.

That large-scale annihilation of matter/antimatter resulted in a stupendous burst of energy in accordance with the equation E = m*c^2, and this is what brought about all that radiation. Our freedom as a single quark was short-lived; in less than a microsecond, two other quarks joined each of us, and together, as a trio of quarks, we got bigger and became a proton or maybe a neutron, with the former having an 80 percent probability and the latter about 20 percent.

Q: Oh, great. So I got some mass with that "God particle" inside of me? The one they call "Higgs boson"?

A: It was the media that called it "God particle". The scientists did not mind the publicity. Actually, it was neither God nor particle; it was a boson, which is a force and not a particle. A proton consists of three quarks (two up quarks and one down quark) and of nothing else but these three quarks. The funny thing is that the proton mass is nearly a hundred times the total mass of the three quarks, even though there is nothing else besides the three quarks in the proton. The three quarks add up to just about 1 percent of the total mass of the proton.

Q: Where does the remaining 99 percent of the mass come from?

A: It's from the strong force that binds the three quarks inside the proton. Try to pull them apart; try to separate them. You need an enormous amount of energy to do that. When you apply the equation E = m*c^2, you know that there is mass over there. So it's a boson and not a particle. Higgs was the scientist who thought of this first in 1964, and so they named it the Higgs boson.

Q: You're joking! You can't get away with that; you say that the mass comes from the force. Now, tell me, where does the force come from?

A: Hmm, I guess there is a field out there in addition to the gravitational field and the electromagnetic field. Let's call it the Higgs field. In this Higgs field, trillions of quarks and antiquarks are arriving and then annihilating each other. In the end, nothing is left except the energy acquired from all the collisions, which becomes the force that binds the quarks that arrive (that is, those quarks that fail to find their antiquarks and thus do not get annihilated).

Q: Such as those inside you and me?

A: Exactly. And when these quarks inside you and me arrived in this eon of the universe, during that first microsecond after the Big Bang, all they did was progress through that Higgs field.

Q: So the mass is actually nothing other than a manifestation of fundamental particles trying to progress through the Higgs field.

A: You are right, I think.

Q: All that is well and good. But actually, that was not the answer I was looking for w.r.t the significance of the equation E = m*c^2.

A: I can only think of one break-away theory to be considered. Einstein warned us about the math. I believe the final computation was something of a dilemma. That the mass of something that actually hits the speed C changes to 1/0, which would create a black hole as far as pure math goes.

Yes, Einstein warned us about the math, when he said, "It's not good to introduce the concept of the mass M = m/(1 – v*v/c*c)^0.5 of a moving body for which no clear definition can be given, and it is better to introduce no other mass concept then the rest mass m0."

Note that even as v gets as much as 85 percent of c, the mass M barely doubles the rest mass. And even at 99 percent of c, it is still about seven times the rest mass. Yes, the final computation was something of a dilemma, and it is better to consider the expression for the momentum and energy of a body in motion, and that as v gets almost equal to c, the square root expression approaches zero and it is the momentum, therefore, that goes toward infinity.

Q: Great, but that's still not the answer I was looking for in regards to the significance of the equation E =m*c^2.

A: Hmmm, I'll try once more.

The equation led to the discovery of fission, which led to the race for supremacy for developing an atomic bomb, which led to the Manhattan Project, the Bombing of Hiroshima and Nagasaki and so on, finally leading to the current situation where we have as many as about 20,000 nuclear warheads on the planet Earth, and not all of them are in possession of safe hands.

And I do believe that the equation E = m*c*c should be used for the development of the world and not its destruction.

Q: So we can add to the list of ideas transmitted by the cosmic mind:

DISMANTLE THE NUCLEAR ARSENAL

AUTHOR'S NOTE

The seminar took place in December 2019, at NIAS Bangalore, in that parallel universe. Let us call that universe 'P' and our own universe 'O'. Events prior to the seminar are assumed similar in both P and O. Video recordings of the seminar were shown on several occasions on TV. They were uploaded on YouTube and were freely available to whoever was interested. Many books would have been written on the subject, and several meetings at the UN and elsewhere would have been held. How effective was the seminar—and its aftermath—in reducing the contamination in the 'Field' and improving peace in the world? I leave the answer to the reader's imagination.

LET US COME BACK TO 'O'.

In this universe, it is the middle of February 2020 as I write this note.

First off, let me provide an update on the 'contamination' of the 'Intelligent Field'.

In a drone strike in early January 2020, the US killed Iranian Gen Qassim Soleimani and shocked the world. The attack was a violation of Iraq's sovereignty and an act of war against Iran. It increased tension and raised the risk of conflict in an already difficult situation. Iran retaliated by firing more than a dozen ballistic missiles at two military bases in Iraq, where American troops were based. As on date, 64 US troops are suffering from traumatic brain injuries. Donald Trump is playing down on these injuries and considers them to be mere headaches.

On 23rd January 2020, the Bulletin of Atomic Scientists placed the Doomsday Emblematic Clock at 100 seconds to midnight.

As stated by the Bulletin of the Atomic Scientists: *"Humanity continues to face two simultaneous existential dangers—nuclear war and climate change—that are compounded by a threat multiplier and cyber-enabled information warfare that undercuts society's ability to respond. The international security situation is dire, not just because these threats exist, but because world leaders have allowed the international political infrastructure for managing them to erode."*

And to top it all, there has been an impeachment inquiry against President Donald Trump. He was impeached by the House, but in the Senate trial, a two-thirds majority was required to vote for his removal as President. The evidence against Trump was so damning that his non-removal would show American lawmakers and Trump's Republican allies, especially, in extremely poor light.

Now there were 100 Senators, 53 Republicans and 47 Democrats.

There was only one truth. Did the senators arrive at a consensus on what it was?

That is the question.

Assuming all brains were wired to a computer and a suitable contraption was used, making it impossible for the senator to remember if he or she was a Democrat or a Republican and assuming further that all 100 senators were perfectly well-informed, intelligent and honest, then the probability that the Democrats arrive at one truth and the Republicans arrive at a different truth is $= (0.5)\,{}^{\wedge}100$— just about as low as that of an aircraft being assembled by a tornado striking a junkyard.

All but one Republican (Mitt Romney) voted against Trump's removal, and Donald Trump was acquitted.

I call it nothing other than 'Tribal Loyalty'.

Now, it can't be that the Republicans were not well-informed on the facts of the case. It can't be that they did not understand the law of the land. It can't be that they were not intelligent enough to be able to analyze and understand what the truth is.

But were they honest? That is the question.

So I call it nothing other than 'Debauchery'.

Now, in this universe, there is no company called the 'Revised Greats Incorporated' at Interlaken Switzerland or anywhere else on the planet, and there was no such seminar held at the National Institute of Advanced Studies, Bangalore. Will there be an actual seminar on what's going wrong on Earth and what should be done to initiate a course correction from 'wrong' to 'right'? This remains to be seen.

It is quite apparent that the time to act is now before it is too late. A seminar on understanding and resolving the conflicts between nations, religions, cultures and the East and the West is now urgent.

Responsible leaders of nations must arrive at the conference, not as members of this or that nation, this or that religion or this or that culture, but as experts who will resolve issues from a neutral perspective and from a human perspective. The 'PUGWASH' group and the 'BULLETIN OF ATOMIC SCIENTISTS' group must play a vital role in facilitating THE CONFERENCE.

Intelligence must conquer the Unintelligence.

This is not my book. It is everyone's book. The 'Unity of Consciousness', the 'One-ness of the mind', the 'Six Words', 'We all have the same mind', the 'Equation of the Upanishads', 'Atman = Brahman', the 'Intelligent Field', the 'Traveling Cosmic Mind', etc., imply that we are all one. But our consciousnesses are in the singular, thus giving each of us individual identities to play our parts in this human drama. I request and urge the common people everywhere to get involved in whatever way they can to help in the continuation of the extraordinary intelligent life on this wonderful planet.

Concerning the 9/11 attacks, every informed person is aware of the deep state's role in it. Possibly, all living Presidents of the US know it. Most world leaders know it. Vladimir Putin knows it and is in possession of satellite pictures in support. Structural engineers and architects of the world know it. Expert pilots of the world know it, and expert lawyers of the world know it. But it is still considered an 'Unpatriotic Conspiracy Theory', even though we cannot discredit the evidence that lies in the statement: "Newton's third law of motion cannot be violated".

Clearly, the evidence is compelling, and it can put the US Attorney in an unenviable position. It can also place the common man in America—particularly the sensitive type—in a terrible predicament, for he has to carry the stigma that he belongs to a nation whose leaders are engaged in stage-managing unnecessary wars. It makes it even worse for him when he realizes that he is paying for all this with his taxes.

With all this, it is unlikely that there will be further investigation into this sordid affair. It is best to forgive and forget and just consider it as an 'aberration' of some kind. However, the least that should happen is the realization—significant awareness—that there is a deep state in America and many other countries that must be taken care of.

On the question of what should be done about the deep states of the world, one has to realize—as explained by Einstein—"that the powerful industrial groups concerned in the manufacture of arms are doing their best in all countries to prevent the peaceful settlement of international disputes". The rulers of some of these countries either do not mind this or do not have adequate control over their armies. But the people of these countries—particularly the younger generation—should understand this and vehemently, yet peacefully, voice their opinion against their leaders as well as the leaders of their armies. In this respect, the fate of the nations hangs on the people themselves; everyone must always bear that in mind.

Finally, in the words of Einstein,

"May the conscience and the common sense of the peoples be awakened, so that we may reach a new stage in the life of nations, where people will look back on war as an incomprehensible aberration of their forefathers."

Deep State is a play about an imaginary conversation at a seminar in a parallel universe. The words spoken by the various characters in the play are either my own or the relevant character's own words from books/articles/quotes. These are very much in the public domain.

Some Examples:

1. *Ideas and Opinions* by Albert Einstein

2. *What is Life* and *Mind and Matter* by Erwin Schrodinger

3. *Some Strangeness in the Proportion* edited by Harry Woolfe

4. *Information and the Nature of Reality* edited by Paul Davies and Gregerson.

5. *Abundance* by Peter Diamantes

6. Articles from the PUGWASH CONFERENCES ON WORLD AFFAIRS group

7. Articles from the BULLETIN OF ATOMIC SCIENTISTS group

8. Newspapers, TV news channels (such as CNN, WION, Al-Jazeera, etc.) and social media

9. *Six Words, Intelligent Field* and *Bright Light In the Sky* by Surendra Kumar Sagar

Deep State: The Mysterious State within the United States is the second of a series of books on the imaginary seminars entitled 'Switched On'. The first book in the series—also under publication—was entitled *Switched On*. The manuscript of the third book in the series, *100 Seconds to Midnight*, is in progress. The central theme of all the books in this series is the same:

> SWITCH OFF the deep states of the nations (especially America), comprising of their vast military-industrial complexes and SWITCH ON the good times for the people of the world. The main difference in the books is that the imaginary seminars are held at different times and capture the latest on the significant events in these fast-changing geo-politics on the planet.

ACKNOWLEDGMENTS

First off, I am deeply indebted to Prof. M.S. Swaminathan, the ex-president of the Pugwash Conferences on World Affairs, for his excellent review of the first book in the series, *Switched On*. Incidentally, Prof Swaminathan also wrote the foreword for my earlier book, *Intelligent Field*.

Some of the participants (characters) in the imaginary seminar are friends (in this universe) who have interacted via email with me. The words spoken by them in the play are the same as the words they wrote in their emails. Special thanks are due to Mr. A.K. Chandrashekhar and Dr. Clifton K. Meador for their significant contribution in this regard. Some others in this list include Lt. Gen Arjun Ray, Dharmesh Misra and Nitish Bhat, to name just a few. The list is exhaustive, and I do apologize for not mentioning all names here. Nevertheless, I thank them all for their words.

Thanks to my lovely artist wife, Bharati Sagar, for her unstinted support. Her exhibition of paintings entitled 'Intelligence in the Field' held at Galerie De'Arts, Bangalore in October 2016 and another exhibition of 26 abstract paintings on the intelligent field held at the gallery, Time and Space, in November 2017, were major success stories. I expect her to hold a similar one on *Deep State*. Her painting, Conversations at a Seminar, showing John Wheeler and Eugene Wigner in conversation, is on the cover of this book.

Thanks to my sons, Kamal Sagar and Nikhil Sagar, for their help and support. Thanks to Sumit Chowdhury for his help and contribution to the development of this book. I thank the dedicated team at Notion Press Publishers for a very professional job done in editing, cover design as well as interior design and layout of the book.

TOP OF FORM

PRAISE FOR SAGAR AND HIS BOOKS

SWITCHED ON

"This is the book we have been waiting for. It is a significant attempt toward developing a better understanding of the deep state of America and that of many other countries. These deep states are able to stage-manage nearly every war on Earth in a way that ensures business as usual for their vast military-industrial complexes. Together, these deep states are all set to create war fronts at several locations on the planet, never mind if the common people of these warring countries do not want war. The author makes a valiant attempt to awaken the conscience and common sense of human beings so that we can 'dismantle' these deep states of the world and reach a new stage in our lives where we can look back on war as an incomprehensible aberration of our past."

– Prof. M.S. Swaminathan, Founder Chairman and Chief Mentor of UNESCO, Chair in Eco Technology, M.S. Swaminathan Research Foundation, Ex-President of Pugwash Conferences on Science and World Affairs.

"At the outset, I wish to mention that Sagar's latest book, unlike his previous books (stressing on the scientific aspects of cosmology and the place of mind in the universe), concentrates on the geo-politics of the "deep states" and "Military-Industrial Complex (MIC)" in the US, in particular, and in other nations in general. The first half of the full text explains how the deep states and MIC work in parallel to national governments to thwart all efforts by all concerned to bring about a peaceful resolution of all intra and international civil, political, social, economic, ethnoreligious, ecological and other conflicts.

What is more, they indeed acerbate such conflicts to such a pitch as to increase the danger of nuclear warfare or ecological Armageddon in the near future to near certainty. In particular, the deep states and MIC of the US, Russia and China enhance the risk of nuclear war far more than those of other nations. This endangers the continued survival and evolution of mind alone, not only alone on Earth but prevents the opportunity near at hand for mind on Earth to integrate with and ride piggy-back on a universe-wide mind possibly in existence at a higher stage of evolution than ours.

The second half of the text tries to find a solution to the problems created by the deep states and MIC so that the mind on Earth is freed to evolve along its path in a smooth and uncluttered manner. Sagar's bringing in the whole text in the style of Greek dialogues between "revised versions" or reincarnations of path-breaking scientists and philosophers of the past tries to add spice to the issues under discussion without in any way allowing the seriousness of the discussion to sag in any way.

The conclusions, though fuzzy, cannot but be otherwise in an attempt to read and, if possible, alter the future of humanity and the universal mind toward its best glory. If this book, during its publication, can reach leaders of all the nuclear nations and nations with vast MICs and the representatives of all other member nations of the UNGA, one hopes there is a chance, however slender, that the Earth-wide mind is set on its evolutionary path toward uncluttered improvement to its fullest potential.

This chance singularly justifies all his painstaking efforts in bringing out the book. I wish all success to the book while hoping it has the widest possible reach among those who are concerned about peace and progress on Earth as also among those who wittingly or unwittingly are threats to such peace and progress so that both their minds are reoriented to merge and move together in unison from here onwards."

– A.K. Chandrashekhar, Retired Finance Executive with interest in Science, Philosophy and Social Wellbeing.

BRIGHT LIGHT IN THE SKY

"Surendra Kumar Sagar's third book, *Bright Light In The Sky,* follows the trajectory of his earlier books in being profound, provocative and probing. Reading Mr. Sagar's latest contribution, I am reminded of Edward Gibbon's

Decline and Fall of the Roman Empire, which is a narrative through a thousand years. We see the greatness of that empire at its height, its military organization, its provincial administration, its welter of races, the rise and clash of two religions, the passage of Greek philosophy into Christian theology.

But throughout this 'history', it is Gibbon who speaks. Mr. Sagar's saga resonates with similar vibrations. The ideas, events and instances described in his book are not his creation. But the voice you hear is the inimitable Surendra Kumar Sagar weaving a tapestry of thought and philosophy, ushering a grand confluence of ideas and conundrums, displaying the need for convergence of imagination as a compass for our elusive quest for a sense of the future, on the journey yet to be."

**– Shoumen Palit Austin Datta, Director of MIT,
Academician, Author and Research Scientist at MIT**

"I am very happy to learn about your new book. It is a very interesting one. I wish you continued success in achieving a nuclear peril free world."

**– Prof. M.S. Swaminathan, Founder Chairman and
Chief Mentor of UNESCO, Chair in EcoTechnology,
M.S. Swaminathan Research Foundation**

"This is the third book of Surendra Kumar Sagar, a trilogy on nuclear proliferation, possible nuclear war scenarios, international geo-politics and power games and where the world stands now, all set into a philosophic and scientific background. Mr. Sagar is a structural engineer yet displays a remarkable understanding of the heart of the quantum world, its implications and possible connections with the human mind and consciousness, all via the 'information in the field.'"

– Dr. Ashok Kumar Jain, National Award-winning Nuclear Scientist

"This is a more elaborate and updated version of the similar background given in his earlier two books on the subject. Other than surprise at the doubts expressed on the US findings of the reported 9/11 air attack that brought down the twin towers of the World Trade Center at New York, I endorse most of his views and conclusions on the parade of relevant events recounted. Sagar is more focused on the nuclear landscape and has not given adequate stress on the likelihood of chemical/germ-warfare, climate change and environmental pollution overtaking or combining with nuclear antagonisms between nations to increase the risk and to hasten the end of humanity.

While a nuclear Armageddon may bring about the end virtually instantaneously, the other factors may bring about the end far more lingeringly over a period of decades and/ or years if nothing is done effectively to arrest the trend of movements in respect of these factors or prevent such an Armageddon from happening. It is the world's misfortune now that the US, in particular, and a few other developed nations as well are at the forefront of opposition to climate change.

I wish the book's publication a resounding success and as per schedule at turning nuclear, ecological and other hawks into doves soon enough for the continued survival and evolution of life on Earth."

– A.K. Chandrashekhar, Retired Finance Executive with interest in Science, Philosophy and Social Wellbeing

"Mr. Sagar's third book is a true reflection of his own erudite and eclectic self. Since he is a structural engineer himself, his book presents a cornucopia of fabulously structured thoughts and concepts.

But this is not the structure of a typical engineer with linearity or even multilinearity with right angles and rigid geometric shapes. He presents an intricate, complex and aesthetic organic arabesque of a multilevel forest—with sinuous vines intertwined with massive trunks of giant trees and the shrubs vying for space with ground-level gossamers.

Taking a leap of faith, one could bring in several similes and similarities with our own ancient scriptures. The triumvirate of body, mind and soul is presented in the form of reality, information and the right value system—GOOD SENSE. The psychosomatic interactions are paralleled with the mutual influence of reality and information and the serpentine DNA-like shape of such influences.

And then Mr. Sagar presents the ultimate conundrum—the very survival of Homo sapiens a la Yuval Harari. Through a willowy wizardry of equations, it is predicted that if we, humans, can manage to survive any nuclear holocaust for the next millennia, then we are pretty much assured of perpetual existence.

In his book, Mr. Sagar plumbs the depths of unfathomable profundity and covers an extraordinary canvas of eternal expanses of time and space. Weaving through these unthinkable discontinuities is his very unique concept of the traveling cosmic mind, which is like the unifying force envisaged by quantum physicists and atomic scientists.

It would be extremely interesting to look forward to Mr. Sagar's fourth book after *Six Words, Intelligent Field* and this *Bright Light In The Sky* and wallow once again in a continuum that is simultaneously both intuitive and counter-intuitive!"

– Prof. Shashi Sharma, Visiting Faculty + Trainer + Adviser for ETHICS and CSR; BE (Mech) from MBM Engg College, Jodhpur + MBA from IIM, Ahmedabad + MS from MIT, USA

"*Bright Light In The Sky* is a non-fiction work that has the pace of a Michael Crichton novel in its tonality! A rare feat by the author, Surendra Kumar Sagar! He has brought philosophy and nuclear-geo-politics in a tone of ordinary conversations beautifully! I could not find a single word in the book from start to finish inauthentic in any way. An excellent piece of writing, reminding me of the writings of the Nobel Prize winning mathematician and author, BERTRAND RUSSELL. A masterly putting together of science, astronomy, philosophy and geo-politics! A rare authentic voice! What Sagar has done is taken the complexity of theories of someone like Immanuel Kant's CRITIQUE of PURE REASON and put it in the language of Bertrand Russell!

Congratulations on the brilliant work!"

– Deepak Sinha, Rasa Aur Drama Time, Pune

SIX WORDS

"*Six Words* is an autobiographical epic story—epic in the dictionary sense to mean "extending beyond the usual or ordinary, especially in size or scope". Sagar begins his personal journey at the Big Bang origin of the universe with "I am a quark". He progresses to become an atom of hydrogen, then helium and finally explodes out of a supernova toward Earth as a carbon atom as our planetary system has formed. On Earth, he becomes an organic molecule and after millions of years, he finally becomes a structural engineer.

This book is a tour de force of the major physical sciences, theology and philosophy. Sagar goes deeply into each, explaining in clear terms very complex subjects. The book then moves to a hypothetical seminar in which the major scientists and philosophers gather to compare notes and thinking. Einstein is there along with Erwin Schrodinger, Charles Sherrington, John Wheeler, Eugene

Wigner and many other top scientists from history. This is a major five-star book written by a serious student, thinker and observer of the sciences of the universe. The book's aim is to draw religion and science together in a way that leaves established scientific laws and rules intact. The Six Words do exactly that. I will leave it to the reader to have the joy of uncovering Sagar's *Six Words.*"

– Dr. Clifton K. Meador, Author of the bestselling *Fascinoma*

"...a treatise that ponders the laws of physics, the history of the cosmos, the nature of God and the fate of mankind.

"...kind of "autobiography" of his existence, starting with the formation of his constituent subatomic particles..." "... It begins with a brief, engaging account of cosmology from the Big Bang through the evolution of life. The book then turns to more involved (and less successful) explorations of advanced physics, including the mysteries of Heisenberg's uncertainty principle, "quantum entanglement" and the relativistic paradoxes of travel near the speed of light..."

"... The book's sixth chapter comprises a fanciful "seminar" of great thinkers—from Immanuel Kant to Albert Einstein to contemporary physicist Freeman Dyson..."

"... All this background sets up a section on Sagar's own philosophical speculations, which mix such topics as the anthropic principle—which says that fundamental constants must be able to support the life-forms that observe them—with the quantum mechanics mysticism..."

"...Sagar theorizes that God is an abstract "all intelligent omnipresent...infinite mind"; that humans may eventually merge into the divine "Super-consciousness"; and that our main task is to avoid blowing ourselves up in the next few centuries—a disaster that Sagar considers a near-certainty unless everyone works for world peace."

– Kirkus Reviews

"In *Six Words*, the author, Surendra Kumar Sagar, integrates the works of some of the greatest scientists and thinkers into a discussion in a parallel universe. He fuses quantum physics with psychology to develop a philosophy that brings science and religion together."

– The Hindu

"Words of Wisdom—Science, Philosophy and Religion come together in Surendra Kumar Sagar's fascinating debut, *Six Words*. Sagar uses quantum physics as the backdrop, against which he investigates intricate philosophical questions. Impressive in its scope, *Six Words* discusses some of the most pressing topics of our time, including the existence of a probabilistic universe, the notion of 'one mind' and the meaning of God and Religion. Sagar ultimately manages to raise the question of how humans can come together to change the course of history."

– Bangalore Mirror

INTELLIGENT FIELD

"The present book, *IF*, by Sagar, is in many ways a continuation of his previous work, *Six Words*. The foundations of *IF* may be traced in *Six Words*. Both books present an unusual mix of western philosophy, modern physics and religion in a background of the current world polity. Sagar is a keen observer of events in the international arena and the nuclear stockpile seems to be the main concern, which has the capability to annihilate the humans from the face of the Earth. When there is a weapon available, a situation for its use will arise eventually; this is the source of concern. Unraveling the inner secrets of a nucleus, man captured the ultimate power, which is the source of all energy in the universe. This made him feel invincible. But invincible against whom? It has pitted man against man.

The history of the world is full of wars. Religions have also been used to fight wars and perpetuate conflicts, which severely undermine the modern human values. I may, however, point out that what we call modern human values is deeply engrained in the great philosophies of Eastern religions for ages. These are not new to us in India. But somewhere in the course of history, we lost them in a struggle for survival.

IF lays bare the underlying struggle which is still on in the world in different forms. Sagar raises important questions about the origins and the hidden nature of these perpetual games of power and survival. Are there any unknown dimensions to these questions and happenings?

Sagar is an engineer by profession. But he displays a deep understanding of the heart of modern quantum mechanics, which he has used to propound the concept of the intelligent field. The flow of information in this field keeps everything connected and the evolution of the universe happens in a self-consistent way. Our minds, and the information therein, are also part of this field and therefore, affect each other. This is an interesting concept like a cosmic mind or 'Param Brahma' in the Vedic literature.

The survival of the human race critically depends on the flow of the right kind of information in the field. The IF itself may not have any intentions or motives. It cannot, therefore, ensure our survival. It is the information that we put in the field and the way we interact will probably decide the future course of humans. This is where the author tries to make a vehement appeal to all those in the know of things to attempt to save our extinction. It puts the concepts of mind, consciousness and soul into focus and compels us to think about the motives of our existence and 'if' there is any deeper meaning to it.

Keeping rational thinking and science at the top, it tries to ponder on the ways of merging science with religions of the world. In other words, it argues that what we need is a scientific, religious philosophy to save us from the impending nuclear catastrophe. It is a highly readable book with a large number of original references and cross-references to support the ideas presented by the author. It is remarkable that the author has been able to convey his ideas in simple words even though they may appear weird at times. Sagar has persistently pursued these ideas for many decades and the book represents the essence of his thinking and possible solutions to the problems that mankind faces. It is sure to make its mark in the world."

– Prof. Ashok Kumar Jain, Award-winning Nuclear Physicist And Ex-Head of the Physics Dept, I.I.T. Roorkee

"*Intelligent Field*, by the immensely gifted author, Surendra Kumar Sagar, is a mind-expanding look at what he refers to as the intelligent field, a sort of traveling cosmic mind that controls nature. But it's the 'information' in the field and the flow of such information in the field that is responsible for everything that happens in the universe, including the imparting of intelligence to the field. As mentioned in the Foreword of the book, within this 'intelligent field' is a universal mind that gives us 'consciousness'.

Intelligent Field is a follow-up, of sorts, to Sagar's book, *Six Words*. Both *Intelligent Field* and *Six Words* have a cross-disciplinary approach and are deeply philosophical. In *Intelligent Field*, as in *Six Words*, a wide variety of topics get incorporated into a heady mix, with Sagar always optimistic in the potential for the human race but also pointing out how events unfolding in the United States and globally could lead to the possible end of human life on Earth.

Sagar is not a prophet of gloom and doom in *Intelligent Field*, but he does mention that humans are getting closer and closer to midnight, as far as the doomsday clock goes. There is still time left to pull humanity back from the brink of potential extinction, but it can only be accomplished only if certain measures are taken before it is too late.

In part, *Intelligent Field* is a snapshot in time, presenting a picture of the state of humanity in the time before Donald Trump was elected president of the United States. Sagar writes about the potential that humans can achieve, and also the very real possibility that they might be hurtling toward self-destruction. However, Sagar writes in chapter 1B, "An Integrated Approach Toward Convergence", about how mankind can change the course it is on, through avoiding nuclear war, a convergence of religion with science, resolving conflicts between nations and within nations and eliminating nuclear threat, altogether.

Albert Einstein and Bertrand Russell were two of the main people behind the start of the Pugwash Conferences, which, as Sagar discusses at some length, began in 1957 and were attended by scientists, scholars and public figures desiring to figure out ways to avoid armed conflicts and seek solutions for global problems. Later, nuclear scientist, Joseph Rotblat, was another of the important proponents of the Pugwash Conferences, dedicating his life, as Sagar writes, "to peace and the prevention of nuclear wars".

Some of the other topics Sagar writes about in *Intelligent Field* are the possibility of how the traveling cosmic mind is linked with relativity, entropy, quantum entanglement and, in the philosophical sense, linked with Einstein's cosmic religious feeling. There is also an in-depth discussion on mind, consciousness and the soul, and on the importance of 'information' in defining reality. Sagar also revisits his previous book, *Six Words*, and includes comments and correspondence he has had with others about the book.

Intelligent Field by Surendra Kumar Sagar is a mixture of philosophy, science, religion and rational thinking, a perfect book for anyone who enjoys pondering the answers to life's "Big Questions" and what direction humanity is headed toward. It is also a must-read for fans of Sagar's book, *Six Words*. *Intelligent Field* is destined to become a classic, a book that is sure to make a valuable addition to your reading lists and personal libraries."

– Douglas. R. Cobb (Bestsellersworld.com)